cook's library

pasta and italian

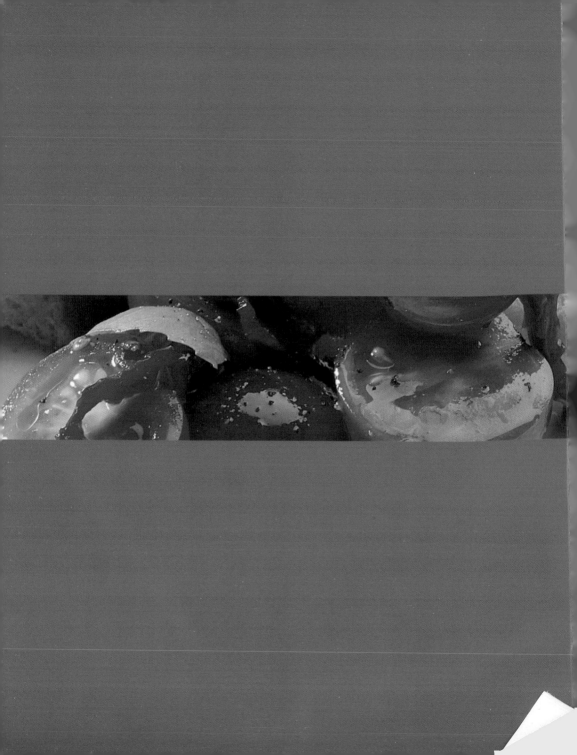

cook's library

pasta and italian

a collection of mouthwatering meals

p

This is a Parragon Book
This edition published in 2005

Parragon
Queen Street House
4 Queen Street
Bath BA1 1HE, UK

ISBN: 1-40544-626-9

Printed in Indonesia

NOTE

This book uses metric and imperial measurements. Follow the same
units of measurement throughout; do not mix metric and imperial.
All spoon measurements are level: teaspoons are assumed to be 5 ml,
and tablespoons are assumed to be 15 ml. Unless otherwise stated,
milk is assumed to be full fat, eggs and individual vegetables such as
potatoes are medium, and pepper is freshly ground black pepper.

The times given for each recipe are an approximate guide only because the
preparation times may differ according to the techniques used by different
people and the cooking times may vary as a result of the type of oven used.
The preparation times include chilling and marinating times, where appropriate.

Recipes using raw or very lightly cooked eggs should be
avoided by infants, the elderly, pregnant women, convalescents,
and anyone suffering from an illness.

Contents

Introduction

Italian food, including the many pasta dishes, pizzas and risottos, is enjoyed all around the world. This inspirational cookbook aims to bring a little bit of Italy into your kitchen!

Glorious sunlight, spectacular beaches, luscious countryside, rugged mountains, world-famous museums and art galleries, elegant designer shops, picturesque villages and magnificent cities – if this were not enough, Italy also boasts one of the longest and finest culinary traditions in the whole of Europe.

The ancient Romans loved good food and plenty of it, vying with each other to produce increasingly lavish and outlandish banquets. One of the earliest cookbooks was written by Apicius, a gourmet in the first century. Overseas trade, as the Roman Empire expanded, brought new ingredients, and agriculture began to flourish at home. And wine production was just as prodigious as it is today.

With the collapse of the Roman Empire, the diet of the region returned to plainer fare, relying mainly on the wealth of cereals, fruit and vegetables that could be cultivated on the fertile plains. However, with the Renaissance, an interest in and enthusiasm for fine food revived and, once again, the fashionable and wealthy presided over extravagant banquets when entertaining friends.

Italian pastry cooks were valued throughout the courts of Europe and were generally acknowledged as the best in the world. When Catherine de Medici went to Paris to marry the future King Henri II in 1533, she took an army of Italian cooks with her and changed French culinary traditions irrevocably. A new middle class developed who also took an interest in eating well, creating a bourgeois cuisine characterized by fresh flavours and simple, unsauced dishes. The poor, of course, continued with their peasant subsistence.

The very finest produce and freshest ingredients still characterise Italian cuisine as a whole. Although modern transportation makes it possible for more exotic ingredients to travel across the world, Italian cooking still centres on home-grown produce. Over 60 per cent of the land is devoted to crops and pasture. With a climate that ranges from very cold in the Alps and Apennines to semi-tropical along the coast of the Ligurian Sea, the range of produce is extensive: olives, oranges, lemons, figs, grapes pomegranates, almonds, wheat, potatoes, tomatoes, sugar beet, maize and rice.

Livestock includes cattle and buffalo, sheep, goats, pigs and chickens. In a single year, Italy produces nearly 6.5 million tonnes of wine, nearly 2.5 million tonnes of olives, about 500,000 tonnes of olive oil, over 4.5 million tonnes of tomatoes and 120 million chickens.

The introduction to this book continues to explore Italy, region by region, to discover the different types of food that are identified with specific areas of the country. Seasonal ingredients are also examined to provide the reader with an insight into the type of produce used by the very discerning people of Italy.

Ragu Sauce

3 tbsp olive oil
45 g/1½ oz butter
2 large onions, chopped
4 celery sticks, sliced thinly
175 g/6 oz streaky bacon, chopped
2 garlic cloves, chopped
500 g/1 lb 2 oz minced lean beef
2 tbsp tomato purée
1 tbsp flour
400 g/14 oz can chopped tomatoes
150 ml/¼ pint beef stock
150 ml/¼ pint red wine
2 tsp dried oregano
½ tsp freshly grated nutmeg
salt and pepper

1 Heat the oil and butter in a saucepan over a medium heat. Add the onions, celery and bacon and fry for 5 minutes, stirring.

2 Stir in the garlic and minced beef and cook, stirring until the meat has lost its redness. Lower the heat and cook for 10 minutes, stirring.

3 Increase the heat to medium, stir in the tomato purée and the flour and cook for 1–2 minutes. Stir in the tomatoes, stock and wine and bring to the boil, stirring. Season and stir in the oregano and nutmeg. Cover and simmer for 45 minutes, stirring occasionally. The sauce is now ready to use.

Basic Pasta Dough

550 g/1 lb 4 oz durum wheat flour
4 eggs, lightly beaten
1 tbsp olive oil
salt

1 Lightly flour a work surface. Sift the flour with a pinch of salt into a mound. Make a well in the centre and add the eggs and oil.

2 Using a fork or your fingertips, gradually work the mixture until the ingredients are combined. Knead vigorously for 10–15 minutes.

3 Set the dough aside to rest for 25 minutes, before rolling it out as thinly and evenly as possible and cutting to the required shape.

Pasta may be coloured and flavoured with extra ingredients that are usually added with the beaten egg:

Black	add 1 tsp squid or cuttlefish ink.
Green	add 125 g/4 oz well-drained, cooked spinach.
Purple	work 1 large, cooked beetroot in a food processor and add with 55 g/ 2 oz extra flour.
Red	add 2 tbsp tomato purée.

Regional Cooking

To talk about Italian cuisine is somewhat misleading, as it is not a single entity. The country has been united only since 17 March, 1861 and Italians still have a powerful sense of their regional identity. Regional cuisine is a source of pride and considerable competition. Sicilians are dismissed as *mangimaccaroni* (pasta eaters), while they express their contempt for Neapolitan cooking with the term *mangiafoglie* (vegetable eaters). Each region bases its cuisine on local ingredients, so the best ham comes from the area where pigs are raised, fish and seafood feature in coastal regions, butter is used in dishes from the north of Italy where there is dairy farming, while olive oil is characteristic of southern recipes.

Abruzzi & Molise

This was once a single region and although it has now been divided into two separate provinces, they remain closely associated. Located in northern Italy to the east of Rome, the area is well known for its high-quality cured meats and cheese. The cuisine is traditional and also features lamb and fish and seafood in the coastal areas. Peperoncino, a tiny, fiery hot, dried red chilli, is from Abruzzi.

Basilicata

If the Italian peninsula looks like a boot, Basilicata is located on the arch of the foot. The landscape is rugged and inhospitable, with much of the region being over 2,000 metres/6,500 feet above sea level. It is hardly surprising, therefore, that the cuisine is warming and filling, with many recipes for substantial soups. Cured meats, pork, lamb and game are typical ingredients and freshwater fish are abundant in the more mountainous areas.

Calabria

In the south, on Italy's toe, Calabria is a region of dramatic contrasts – superb beaches and towering mountains. Excellent fish and seafood typify the local cuisine, which is well known for its swordfish and tuna dishes. Fruit and vegetables are abundant, particularly oranges, lemons, aubergines and olives. Like other southern regions, desserts are a speciality, often based on local figs, honey or almonds.

Campania

Naples on the west coast is the home of pizza, now known across the world from Sydney to New York, and the region bases many of its other dishes on the wonderful sun-ripened tomatoes grown locally. Fish and seafood feature strongly in the Neapolitan diet and robust herb-flavoured stews, redolent with garlic, are popular. Pastries and fruit desserts are also characteristic.

Emilia-Romagna

A central Italian province, Emilia-Romagna's capital is the beautiful medieval city of Bologna, nicknamed *la grassa*, the fat city, and home to some of the best restaurants in the country.

A gourmet paradise, the region is famous for Parmesan cheese and Parma ham from Parma, balsamic vinegar from the area around Modena, cotechino, mortadella and other cured meats and, of course, spaghetti alla bolognese. Butter, cream and other dairy products feature in the fine food of the region and a wide range of pasta dishes is popular.

Lazio

Capital of the region and the country, Rome is a cosmopolitan and sophisticated city with some of the best restaurants – and ice cream parlours – in Europe. Fruit and vegetables are abundant and lamb and veal dishes are typical of the region, which is famous for saltimbocca which, because it's so delicious means "jump in the mouth". Here, they have perfected the art of preparing high-quality ingredients in simple, but delicious ways that retain the individual flavours. A Roman speciality is *suppli al telefono* (telephone wires) –

mozzarella cheese wrapped in balls of cooked rice and deep-fried. The mozzarella is stringy, hence the name of the dish.

Liguria

A northern province with a long coastline, Liguria is well known for its superb fish and seafood. It is also said to produce the best basil in Italy and it is where pesto sauce was first invented. The ancient port of Genoa was one of the first places in Europe to import Asian spices and highly seasoned dishes are still characteristic of this area.

Lombardy

An important rice-growing region in north-west Italy, this is the home of risotto with many variations of this dish. Lombardy is credited with the invention of butter, as well as mascarpone cheese. Vegetable soups, stews and pot roasts are characteristic of this region. Bresaola, cured raw beef, is a local speciality that is often served wrapped around a locally produced soft goat's cheese.

Marche

With its long coastline and high mountains, this region is blessed with both abundant seafood and game. Pasta, pork and olives are also commonly found on many menus. The methods of preparation of the fish and seafood and game dishes are also more elaborate than those of neighbouring Umbria.

Piedmont

On the borders of France and Switzerland, Piedmont in the north-west is strongly influenced by its neighbours. A fertile, arable region, it is well known for rice, polenta and gnocchi and is said to grow the finest onions in Italy. Gorgonzola, one of the world's greatest cheeses, comes from this region although, sadly, the village that gave it its name has now been subsumed by the urban sprawl of Milan. Piedmontese garlic is said to be the best in Italy and the local white truffles are a gourmet's dream.

Puglia

On the heel of Italy, this region produces excellent olives, herbs, vegetables and fruit, particularly melons and figs. Fish and seafood are abundant because of its proximity to the coast and fishing ports and the region is known for its oyster and mussel dishes. Calzone, a sort of inside out pizza, was invented here.

Sardinia

This Mediterranean island is famous for its luxurious desserts and extravagant pastries, many of them featuring honey, nuts and home-grown fruit. Hardly surprisingly, fish and seafood – tuna, eel, mullet, sea bass, lobster and mussels – are central to Sardinian cuisine and spit-roasted suckling pig is the national dish served on feast days. Sardo is a mild-tasting pecorino cheese produced in Sardinia.

Sicily

Like their southern neighbours, Sicilians have a sweet tooth, which they indulge with superb cakes, desserts and ice cream, often incorporating locally grown almonds, pistachios and citrus fruits. Pasta dishes are an important part of the diet and fish and seafood, including tuna, swordfish and mussels, feature prominently.

Trentino Alto-Adige

A mountainous region in the north-east, Trentino has been strongly influenced by its Austrian neighbour. Smoked sausage and dumplings are characteristic of the region, which is also well known for its filled pasta dishes.

Tuscany

The fertile plains of Tuscany are ideal for farming and the region produces superb fruit and vegetables. Cattle are raised here and both steak and veal dishes feature on the Tuscan menu, together with a wide range of game. Tripe is a local speciality and Panforte di Siena, a traditional Christmas cake made with honey and nuts, comes from the city of Siena. A grain known as farro is grown almost exclusively in Tuscany, where it is used to make a nourishing soup.

Umbria

Pork, lamb, game and freshwater fish, prepared and served simply,

but deliciously, characterise the excellent cuisine of the region. Fragrant black truffles, the "black gold of Italy", are a feature and Umbrian cooking makes good use of its high-quality olive oil. Umbria is also famous for imbrecciata, a hearty soup made with lentils, chick-peas and haricot beans.

Veneto and Friuli

An intensively farmed area in the north-east of Italy, this region produces cereals and almost 20 per cent of the country's wine. Polenta and risotto feature in the cuisine, as well as an extensive range of fish and seafood. Risi e bisi, rice and peas, is a dish which was served every year at the Doge's banquet in Venice to honour the city's patron saint, Mark.

Basic Recipes

These recipes form the basis of several of the dishes contained throughout this book. Many of these basic recipes can be made in advance and stored in the refrigerator until required.

Basic Tomato Sauce

2 tbsp olive oil
1 small onion, chopped
1 garlic clove, chopped
400 g/14 oz can chopped tomatoes
2 tbsp chopped fresh parsley
1 tsp dried oregano
2 bay leaves
2 tbsp tomato purée
1 tsp sugar
salt and pepper

1 Heat the oil in a saucepan over a medium heat and fry the onion for 2–3 minutes or until translucent. Add the garlic and fry for 1 minute.

2 Stir in the chopped tomatoes, parsley, oregano, bay leaves, tomato purée, sugar, and salt and pepper to taste.

3 Bring the sauce to the boil, then simmer, uncovered, for 15–20 minutes or until the sauce has reduced by half. Taste the sauce and adjust the seasoning if necessary. Discard the bay leaves just before serving.

Béchamel Sauce

300 ml/10 fl oz milk
2 bay leaves
3 whole cloves
1 small onion
55 g/2 oz, butter
45 g/1½ oz flour
300 ml/10 fl oz single cream
large pinch of freshly grated nutmeg
salt and pepper

1 Press the cloves into the onion. Place in a small non-stick saucepan with the milk and bay leaves and bring the milk to the boil. Remove from the heat.

2 Strain the milk into a jug and rinse the saucepan. Melt the butter in the saucepan and stir in the flour. Stir for 1 minute, then gradually pour in the milk, stirring constantly. Cook for 3 minutes, then pour in the cream and bring to the boil, stirring constantly. Remove from the heat and season with nutmeg, salt and pepper to taste.

Lamb Sauce

2 tbsp olive oil
1 large onion, sliced
2 celery sticks, thinly sliced
500 g/1 lb 2 oz lean lamb, minced
3 tbsp tomato purée
150 g/5½ oz bottled sun-dried tomatoes, drained and chopped
1 tsp dried oregano
1 tbsp red wine vinegar
150 ml/5 fl oz chicken stock
salt and pepper

1 Heat the oil in a frying pan over a medium heat and fry the onion and celery until the onion is translucent, about 3 minutes. Add the lamb and fry, stirring frequently, until it browns.

2 Stir in the tomato purée, sun-dried tomatoes, oregano, vinegar and stock. Season with salt and pepper to taste.

3 Bring the sauce to the boil and cook, uncovered, for 20 minutes or until the meat has absorbed the stock. Taste and adjust the seasoning if necessary.

Espagnole Sauce

2 tbsp butter
25 g/1 oz plain flour
1 tsp tomato purée
250 ml/9 fl oz hot veal stock
1 tbsp Madeira
1½ tsp white wine vinegar
2 tbsp olive oil
25 g/1 oz bacon, diced
25 g/1 oz carrot, diced
25 g/1 oz onion, diced
15 g/½ oz celery, diced
15 g/½ oz leek, sliced
15 g/½ oz fennel, diced
1 fresh thyme sprig
1 bay leaf

1 Melt the butter in a non-stick saucepan, add the flour and cook, stirring, until lightly coloured. Add the tomato purée, then stir in the hot veal stock, Madeira and white wine vinegar. Cook for 2 minutes.

2 Heat the oil in a separate saucepan. Add the bacon, carrot, onion, celery, leek, fennel, thyme sprig and bay leaf and fry until the vegetables have softened. Remove the vegetables from the saucepan with a slotted spoon and drain thoroughly. Add to the sauce and simmer for 4 hours, stirring occasionally. Strain the sauce before using.

Cheese Sauce

25 g/1 oz butter
1 tbsp flour
250 ml/9 fl oz milk
2 tbsp single cream
pinch of freshly grated nutmeg
45 g/1½ oz mature Cheddar, grated
1 tbsp freshly grated Parmesan
salt and pepper

1 Melt the butter in a non-stick saucepan, stir in the flour and cook for 1 minute. Gradually pour in the milk, stirring all the time. Stir in the cream and season the sauce with nutmeg, salt and pepper to taste.

2 Simmer the sauce for 5 minutes to reduce, then remove it from the heat and stir in the cheeses. Stir until the cheeses have melted and blended into the sauce.

Italian Red Wine Sauce

150 ml/5 fl oz Brown Stock
   (see page 16)
150 ml/5 fl oz Espagnole Sauce
   (see left)
125 ml/4 fl oz red wine
2 tbsp red wine vinegar
4 tbsp shallots, chopped
1 bay leaf
1 thyme sprig
pepper

1 First make a demi-glace sauce: combine the Brown Stock and Espagnole Sauce in a saucepan and heat for 10 minutes, stirring occasionally.

2 Meanwhile, put the red wine, red wine vinegar, shallots, bay leaf and thyme in a saucepan, bring to the boil and cook until it is reduced by three-quarters.

3 Strain the demi-glace sauce and add to the saucepan containing the Red Wine Sauce. Leave to simmer for 20 minutes, stirring occasionally. Season with pepper to taste and strain the sauce before using.

Brown Stock

900 g/2 lb veal bones and shin of beef
1 leek, sliced
1 onion, chopped
1 celery stick, sliced
1 carrot, sliced
1 bouquet garni
150 ml/5 fl oz white wine vinegar
1 thyme sprig
1.75 litres/3 pints cold water

1 Roast the veal bones and shin of beef in their own juices in the oven for 40 minutes.

2 Transfer the bones to a large saucepan, add the leek, onion, celery, carrot, bouquet garni, white wine vinegar and thyme and cover with the cold water. Simmer over a very low heat for about 3 hours. Strain and blot the fat from the surface with kitchen paper before using, or refrigerate to remove the fat easily.

Fish Stock

900 g/2 lb non-oily fish pieces, such as heads, tails, trimmings and bones
150 ml/5 fl oz white wine
1 onion, chopped
1 carrot, sliced
1 celery stick, sliced
4 black peppercorns
1 bouquet garni
1.75 litres/3 pints water

1 Put the fish pieces, wine, onion, carrot, celery, black peppercorns, bouquet garni and water in a large saucepan and leave to simmer for 30 minutes, stirring occasionally. Strain and blot the fat from the surface with kitchen paper before using.

Italian Cheese Sauce

2 tbsp butter
25 g/1 oz plain flour
300 ml/10 fl oz hot milk
pinch of nutmeg
pinch of dried thyme
2 tbsp white wine vinegar
3 tbsp double cream
55 g/2 oz mozzarella cheese, grated
55 g/2 oz Parmesan cheese, grated
1 tsp English mustard
2 tbsp soured cream
salt and pepper

1 Melt the butter in a saucepan and stir in the flour. Cook, stirring, over a low heat until the roux is light in colour and crumbly in texture. Stir in the hot milk and cook, stirring, for 15 minutes until thick and smooth.

2 Add the nutmeg, thyme, white wine vinegar and season to taste. Stir in the cream and mix well.

3 Stir in the cheeses, mustard and soured cream and mix until the cheeses have melted and blended into the sauce.

How to Use This Book

Each recipe contains a wealth of useful information, including a breakdown
of nutritional quantities, preparation and cooking times, and level of difficulty.
All of this information is explained in detail below.

A full-colour photograph
of the finished dish.

The Italian name for this
dish, Saltimbocca, means
'jump into the mouth'
because its so delicious.
The stuffed rolls are quick
and easy to make.

Saltimbocca

SERVES 4

4 turkey fillets or 4 veal escalopes,
 about 450 g/1 lb in total
100 g/3½ oz Parma ham
8 fresh sage leaves
1 tbsp olive oil
1 onion, finely chopped
200 ml/7 fl oz white wine
200 ml/7 fl oz chicken stock

1 Place the turkey or veal between sheets of greaseproof paper. Pound the
meat with a meat mallet or the end of a rolling pin to flatten it slightly. Cut
each escalope in half.

2 Trim the Parma ham to fit each piece of turkey or veal and place over the
meat. Lay a sage leaf on top. Roll up the escalopes and secure the rolls with a
cocktail stick.

3 Heat the oil in a frying pan and cook the onion for 3–4 minutes. Add the
turkey or veal rolls to the pan and cook for 5 minutes, or until brown all over.

4 Pour the wine and stock into the pan and leave to simmer for 15 minutes if
using turkey, and 20 minutes for veal, or until tender. Serve immediately.

The method is clearly
explained with step-by-
step instructions that
are easy to follow.

The ingredients for
each recipe are listed
in the order that they
are used.

The nutritional
information provided
for each recipe is per
serving or per portion.
Optional ingredients,
variations or serving
suggestions have not
been included in the
calculations.

NUTRITION
Calories 303; Sugars 0.3 g; Protein 29 g;
Carbohydrate 1 g; Fat 17 g; Saturates 1 g

moderate
15 mins
25–30 mins

COOK'S TIP

If using turkey rather than veal, watch it carefully as turkey tends to turn dry
very quickly if overcooked.

Cook's tips provide useful
information regarding
ingredients or cooking
techniques.

The number of stars represents the
difficulty of each recipe, ranging from
very easy (1 star) to challenging (4 stars).

This amount of time represents the
preparation of ingredients, including
cooling, chilling and soaking times.

This represents the cooking time.

Soups

Soups are an important part of the Italian cuisine. They vary in consistency from light and delicate to hearty main meal soups. Texture is always apparent – Italians rarely serve smooth soups. Some may be partially puréed but the identity of the ingredients is never entirely obliterated. There are regional characteristics, too. In the north, soups are often based on rice, while in Tuscany, thick bean- or bread-based soups are popular. Tomato, garlic and pasta soups are typical of the south. Minestrone is known world-wide, but the authentic version originates from Milan – all versions are full of vegetables and are delicious and satisfying. Fish soups also abound in one guise or another in coastal areas, and most of these are village specialities, producing varieties that are always bursting with flavour.

This soup is best made with white onions, which have a milder flavour than the more usual brown variety. If you cannot get hold of them, try using large Spanish onions instead.

Tuscan Onion Soup

SERVES 4

50 g/1³/₄ oz pancetta ham, diced
1 tbsp olive oil
4 large white onions, sliced thinly in rings
3 garlic cloves, chopped
850 ml/1¹/₂ pints hot chicken or ham stock
4 slices ciabatta or other Italian bread
50 g/1³/₄ oz butter
75 g/2³/₄ oz Gruyère or Cheddar cheese, coarsely grated
salt and pepper

1 Dry fry the pancetta in a large saucepan for 3–4 minutes, or until it begins to brown. Remove the pancetta from the pan and set aside until required.

2 Add the oil to the pan and cook the onions and garlic over a high heat for 4 minutes. Reduce the heat, cover and cook for 15 minutes, or until they are lightly caramelized.

3 Add the stock to the saucepan and bring to the boil. Reduce the heat and leave the mixture to simmer, covered, for about 10 minutes.

4 Toast the slices of ciabatta on both sides, under a preheated grill, for 2–3 minutes, or until golden. Spread the ciabatta with butter and top with the Gruyère or Cheddar cheese. Cut the bread into bite-sized pieces.

5 Add the reserved pancetta to the soup and season to taste with salt and pepper. Pour into 4 soup bowls and top with the toasted bread.

NUTRITION

Calories 390; Sugars 0g; Protein 9g; Carbohydrate 15 g; Fat 33 g; Saturates 14 g

⭐ very easy
🕐 5–10 mins
🕐 40–45 mins

 COOK'S TIP

Pancetta is similar to bacon, but it is air- and salt-cured for about 6 months. It is available from most delicatessens and some large supermarkets. If you cannot obtain pancetta, use unsmoked bacon instead.

A thick and creamy soup that is based on a traditional Tuscan recipe. If you use dried beans, the preparation and cooking times will be longer.

Tuscan Bean Soup

1 If you are using canned beans, drain them thoroughly and reserve the liquid. If you are using dried beans that have been soaked overnight, drain them thoroughly. Bring a large pan of water to the boil, add the beans and boil for 10 minutes. Cover the pan and simmer for a further 30 minutes or until tender. Drain the beans, reserving the cooking liquid.

2 Heat the oil in a large frying pan and fry the garlic for 2–3 minutes or until just beginning to brown.

3 Add the beans and 400 ml/14 fl oz of the reserved liquid to the pan, stirring. You may need to add a little water if there is insufficient liquid. Stir in the crumbled stock cube. Bring the mixture to the boil and then remove the pan from the heat.

4 Place the bean mixture in a food processor and blend to form a smooth purée. Alternatively, mash the bean mixture to a smooth consistency. Season to taste with salt and pepper and stir in the milk.

5 Pour the soup back into the pan and gently heat to just below boiling point. Stir in the oregano just before serving.

SERVES 4

800 g/1 lb 12 oz canned butter beans or
   225 g/8 oz dried butter beans, soaked
   overnight,
1 tbsp olive oil
2 garlic cloves, crushed
1 vegetable or chicken stock cube, crumbled
150 ml/5 fl oz milk
2 tbsp chopped fresh oregano
salt and pepper

NUTRITION
Calories 250; Sugars 4 g; Protein 13 g;
Carbohydrate 29 g; Fat 10 g; Saturates 2 g

 very easy

8 hrs 5 mins

 10 mins

This thick, creamy soup has a wonderful, warming golden colour. It is an ideal use for the flesh of your Halloween lantern.

Orange, Thyme *and* Pumpkin Soup

SERVES 4

2 tbsp olive oil
2 medium onions, chopped
2 garlic cloves, chopped
900 g/2 lb pumpkin, peeled and cut into 2.5 cm/1 inch chunks
1.5 litres /2¾ pints boiling vegetable or chicken stock
finely grated rind and juice of 1 orange
3 tbsp fresh thyme, stalks removed
150 ml/5 fl oz milk
salt and pepper
crusty bread, to serve

1 Heat the olive oil in a large saucepan. Add the onions to the saucepan and cook for 3–4 minutes or until softened. Add the garlic and pumpkin and cook for a further 2 minutes, stirring well.

2 Add the boiling vegetable stock, orange rind and juice and 2 tablespoons of the thyme to the saucepan. Leave to simmer, covered, for 20 minutes or until the pumpkin is tender.

3 Place the mixture in a food processor and blend until smooth. Alternatively, mash the mixture with a potato masher until smooth. Season to taste with salt and pepper.

4 Return the soup to the saucepan and add the milk. Reheat the soup for 3–4 minutes or until it is piping hot, but not boiling. Sprinkle with the remaining fresh thyme just before serving.

5 Divide the soup among 4 warm soup bowls and serve with lots of fresh crusty bread.

NUTRITION
Calories *111*; Sugars *4 g*; Protein *2 g*;
Carbohydrate *5 g*; Fat *6 g*; Saturates *2 g*

 very easy

10 mins

35–40 mins

 COOK'S TIP

Pumpkins are usually large vegetables. To make things a little easier, ask the greengrocer to cut a chunk off for you. Alternatively, make double the quantity and freeze the soup for up to 3 months.

This refreshing chilled soup is ideal on a hot day, for al fresco dining.

Artichoke Soup

1 Heat the olive oil in a large saucepan and fry the onion and garlic until just softened.

2 Using a sharp knife, roughly chop the artichoke hearts. Add the artichoke pieces to the onion and garlic mixture in the pan. Pour in the hot vegetable stock, stirring.

3 Bring the mixture to the boil, then reduce the heat and leave to simmer, covered, for about 3 minutes.

4 Place the mixture into a food processor and blend until smooth. Alternatively, push the mixture through a sieve to remove any lumps.

5 Return the soup to the saucepan. Stir the single cream and fresh thyme into the soup.

6 Transfer the soup to a large bowl, cover and leave to chill in the refrigerator for about 3–4 hours.

7 Transfer the chilled soup to individual soup bowls and garnish with strips of sun-dried tomato. Serve with lots of fresh, crusty bread.

SERVES 4

1 tbsp olive oil
1 onion, chopped
1 garlic clove, crushed
800 g/1 lb 12 oz canned artichoke hearts, drained
600 ml/1 pint hot vegetable stock
150 ml/5 fl oz single cream
2 tbsp fresh thyme, stalks removed
2 sun-dried tomatoes, cut into strips
crusty bread, to serve

NUTRITION
Calories 159; Sugars 2 g; Protein 2 g; Carbohydrate 5 g; Fat 15 g; Saturates 6 g

easy

5 mins

15 mins

🍳 COOK'S TIP

Try adding 2 tablespoons of dry vermouth, such as Martini, to the soup in step 5 if you wish.

The Calabrian mountains in southern Italy provide large amounts of wild mushrooms. They are rich in flavour and colour and make a wonderful soup.

Calabrian Mushroom Soup

SERVES 4

2 tbsp olive oil
1 onion, chopped
450 g/1 lb mixed mushrooms, such as ceps, oyster and button
300 ml/10 fl oz milk
850 ml/1½ pints hot vegetable stock
8 slices of rustic bread or French stick
50 g/1¾ oz butter, melted
2 garlic cloves, crushed
75 g/2¾ oz Gruyère cheese, finely grated
salt and pepper

1 Heat the oil in a large frying pan and fry the onion for 3–4 minutes, or until soft and golden.

2 Wipe each mushroom with a damp cloth and cut any large mushrooms into smaller, bite-size pieces.

3 Add the mushrooms to the pan, stirring quickly to coat them well in the oil.

4 Add the milk to the pan, bring to the boil, cover and leave to simmer for about 5 minutes. Gradually stir in the hot vegetable stock.

5 Under a preheated grill, toast the bread on both sides until golden.

6 Mix together the butter and garlic and then spoon generous amounts of the garlic butter over the toast.

7 Place the toast in the bottom of a large tureen or divide it among 4 individual serving bowls and pour over the hot soup. Top with the grated Gruyère cheese and serve at once.

NUTRITION
Calories 452; Sugars 5 g; Protein 15 g;
Carbohydrate 42 g; Fat 26 g; Saturates 12 g

easy

5 mins

20 mins

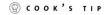 **COOK'S TIP**

Mushrooms absorb liquid, which can lessen the flavour and affect cooking properties. Wipe them with a damp cloth rather than rinsing them in water.

This fresh-tasting soup with green beans, cucumber and watercress can be served warm or chilled on a hot summer's day.

Green Soup

1 Heat the oil in a large saucepan and fry the onion and garlic for 3–4 minutes or until softened. Add the potato and cook for a further 2–3 minutes.

2 Stir in the stock, bring to the boil and leave to simmer for 5 minutes.

3 Add the cucumber to the saucepan and cook for a further 3 minutes or until the potatoes are tender. Test by inserting the tip of a knife into the potato cubes – it should pass through easily.

4 Add the watercress and allow to wilt. Then place the soup in a food processor and blend until smooth. Alternatively, before adding the watercress, mash the soup with a potato masher and push through a sieve, then chop the watercress finely and stir into the soup.

5 Bring a small saucepan of water to the boil and cook the beans for 3–4 minutes or until tender.

6 Add the beans to the soup, season and warm through before serving.

SERVES 4

1 tbsp olive oil
1 onion, chopped
1 garlic clove, chopped
200 g/7 oz potato, peeled and cut into 2.5 cm/1 inch cubes
700 ml/1¼ pints vegetable or chicken stock
1 small cucumber or ½ large cucumber, cut into chunks
85 g/3 oz bunch watercress
125 g/4½ oz green beans, trimmed and halved
salt and pepper

NUTRITION

Calories *121*; Sugars *2 g*; Protein *2 g*; Carbohydrate *10 g*; Fat *8 g*; Saturates *1 g*

easy

5 mins

25–30 mins

👩‍🍳 COOK'S TIP

Try using 125 g/4½ oz mangetouts in this recipe, instead of the beans.

The red kidney beans give this soup a warm glow as well as making it a hearty dish.

Red Bean Soup

SERVES 4

175 g/6 oz dried red kidney beans, soaked overnight
1.7 litres/3 pints water
1 large ham bone or bacon knuckle
2 carrots, chopped
1 large onion, chopped
2 celery sticks, sliced thinly
1 leek, trimmed, washed and sliced
1–2 bay leaves
2 tbsp olive oil
2–3 tomatoes, peeled and chopped
1 garlic clove, crushed
1 tbsp tomato purée
55 g/2 oz arborio or risotto rice
125–175 g/4–6 oz green cabbage, shredded finely
salt and pepper

1 Drain the beans and place them in a saucepan with enough water to cover. Bring to the boil, then boil for 15 minutes to remove any harmful toxins. Skim off any scum on the top. Reduce the heat and simmer for 45 minutes.

2 Drain the beans and put into a clean saucepan with the water, ham bone or knuckle, carrots, onion, celery, leek, bay leaves and olive oil. Bring to the boil, then cover and simmer for 1 hour or until the beans are very tender.

3 Discard the bay leaves and bone, reserving any ham pieces from the bone. Remove a small cupful of the beans and reserve. Purée or liquidize the soup in a food processor or blender, or push through a coarse sieve, and return to a clean saucepan.

4 Add the tomatoes, garlic, tomato purée and rice and season. Bring back to the boil and simmer for about 15 minutes or until the rice is tender.

5 Add the cabbage and reserved beans and ham, and continue to simmer for 5 minutes. Adjust the seasoning and serve very hot. If liked, a piece of toasted crusty bread may be put in the base of each soup bowl before ladling in the soup. If the soup is too thick, add a little boiling water or stock.

NUTRITION
Calories *184*; Sugars *5 g*; Protein *4 g*; Carbohydrate *19 g*; Fat *11 g*; Saturates *2 g*

easy
8 hrs 10 mins
2 hrs 40 mins

A thick vegetable soup which is a delicious meal in itself. Serve with Parmesan cheese and warm sun-dried tomato bread.

Chickpea Soup

1 Heat the oil in a large saucepan, add the leeks and courgettes and cook briskly for 5 minutes, stirring constantly.

2 Add the garlic, tomatoes, tomato purée, bay leaf, chicken stock and chickpeas and stir to mix well.

3 Bring to the boil and simmer for 5 minutes.

4 Shred the spinach finely, add to the soup and cook for 2 minutes. Season to taste with salt and pepper.

5 Discard the bay leaf. Serve the soup immediately with freshly grated Parmesan cheese and warm sun-dried tomato bread.

SERVES 4

2 tbsp olive oil
2 leeks, sliced
2 courgettes, diced
2 garlic cloves, crushed
800 g/1 lb 12 oz canned chopped tomatoes
1 tbsp tomato purée
1 fresh bay leaf
850 ml/1½ pints chicken stock
400 g/14 oz canned chickpeas, drained and rinsed
225 g/8 oz spinach
salt and pepper

to serve
Parmesan cheese, freshly grated
sun-dried tomato bread

NUTRITION
Calories 297; Sugars 0 g; Protein 11 g; Carbohydrate 24 g; Fat 18 g; Saturates 2 g

 very easy

 5 mins

15 mins

🐢 COOK'S TIP

Chickpeas are used extensively in North African cuisine and are also found in Spanish, Middle Eastern and Indian cooking. They have a nutty flavour with a firm texture and canned chickpeas are excellent.

Fresh pesto is a treat to the taste buds and very different in flavour from ready-made pesto. Store fresh pesto in the refrigerator.

Potato *and* Pesto Soup

SERVES 4

3 slices rindless, smoked, fatty bacon, chopped finely
450 g/1 lb floury potatoes, chopped finely
450 g/ 1 lb onions, chopped finely
2 tbsp olive oil
25 g/1 oz butter
600 ml/1 pint chicken stock
600 ml/1 pint milk
100 g/3 ¹/₂ oz dried conchigliette (pasta shells)
150 ml/5 fl oz double cream
chopped fresh parsley
1 quantity Pesto Sauce (see page 133)
salt and pepper

to serve
Parmesan cheese shavings
garlic bread, toasted

1 Fry the bacon in a large saucepan over a medium heat for 4 minutes. Add the olive oil, butter, potatoes and onions and cook for 12 minutes, stirring constantly.

2 Add the stock and milk to the pan, bring to the boil and simmer for 10 minutes. Add the conchigliette and simmer for a further 10–12 minutes.

3 Blend in the cream and simmer for 5 minutes. Add the parsley, salt and pepper and 2 tablespoons of the Pesto Sauce. Transfer the soup to serving bowls and serve with shavings of Parmesan cheese and toasted garlic bread.

NUTRITION
Calories *548*; Sugars *0 g*; Protein *11 g*;
Carbohydrate *10 g*; Fat *52 g*; Saturates *18 g*

easy
15 mins
50 mins

This quick and easy creamy soup has a lovely fresh tomato flavour.

Creamy Tomato Soup

1 Melt the butter in a large saucepan. Add the tomatoes and cook for 5 minutes until the skins start to wrinkle. Season to taste.

2 Add the stock to the saucepan, bring to the boil, cover and simmer for 10 minutes.

3 Meanwhile, under a preheated grill, lightly toast the ground almonds until golden-brown. This will take only 1–2 minutes, so watch them closely.

4 Remove the soup from the heat and place in a food processor and blend the mixture to form a smooth consistency. Alternatively, mash the soup with a potato masher.

5 Pass the soup through a sieve to remove any tomato skin or pips.

6 Place the soup back in the saucepan and return to the heat. Stir in the milk or cream, ground almonds and sugar. Warm the soup through and add the basil just before serving.

7 Transfer the creamy tomato soup to warm soup bowls and serve hot.

SERVES 4

50 g/1¾ oz butter
700 g/1 lb 9 oz ripe tomatoes, preferably plum, roughly chopped
850 ml/1½ pints hot vegetable stock
150 ml/5 fl oz milk or single cream
50 g/1¾ oz ground almonds
1 tsp sugar
2 tbsp shredded fresh basil leaves
salt and pepper

NUTRITION
Calories *218*; Sugars *10 g*; Protein *3 g*;
Carbohydrate *10 g*; Fat *19 g*; Saturates *11 g*

 easy

5 mins

25–30 mins

🖐 **COOK'S TIP**

Very fine breadcrumbs can be used instead of the ground almonds, if you prefer. Toast them in the same way as the almonds and add with the milk or cream in step 6.

Plum tomatoes are ideal for making soups and sauces, as they have denser, less watery flesh than round varieties.

Tomato *and* Pasta Soup

S E R V E S   4

55 g/2 oz unsalted butter
1 large onion, chopped
600 ml/1 pint vegetable stock
900 g/2 lb Italian plum tomatoes, skinned
   and roughly chopped
pinch of bicarbonate of soda
225 g/8 oz dried fusilli
1 tbsp caster sugar
150 ml/5 fl oz double cream
salt and pepper
fresh basil leaves, to garnish
deep-fried croûtons, to serve

1 Melt the butter in a large saucepan, add the onion and fry for 3 minutes. Add half the vegetable stock to the saucepan, with the tomatoes and bicarbonate of soda. Bring the soup to the boil and simmer for 20 minutes.

2 Remove the saucepan from the heat and set aside to cool. Purée the soup in a blender or food processor and pour through a fine sieve back into the rinsed-out saucepan.

3 Add the remaining vegetable stock and the farfalline or spaghetti to the pan, and season to taste with salt and pepper.

4 Add the sugar, bring to the boil, then lower the heat and simmer for about 15 minutes.

5 Pour the soup into a warm tureen, swirl the double cream around the surface of the soup and garnish with fresh basil leaves. Serve immediately, with the croûtons.

N U T R I T I O N
Calories 503; Sugars 16 g; Protein 9 g;
Carbohydrate 59 g; Fat 28 g; Saturates 17 g

easy

5 mins

40 mins

(🍴) **C O O K ' S   T I P**

To make orange and tomato soup, simply use half the quantity of vegetable stock, topped up with the same amount of fresh orange juice, and garnish the soup with orange rind.

A minestra is a soup cooked with pasta; in this case farfalline, a small bow-shaped variety, is used. Served with lentils, this hearty soup is a meal in itself.

Brown Lentil Soup *with* Pasta

1 Place the bacon in a large frying pan together with the onion, garlic and celery. Dry fry for 4–5 minutes, stirring, until the onion is tender and the bacon is just beginning to brown.

2 Add the farfalline to the pan and cook, stirring, for about 1 minute to coat the pasta in the oil.

3 Add the lentils and the stock and bring to the boil. Reduce the heat and leave to simmer for 12–15 minutes, or until the pasta is tender.

4 Remove the pan from the heat and stir in the chopped fresh mint.

5 Transfer the soup to warm soup bowls and serve immediately.

SERVES **4**

4 rashers streaky bacon, cut into small squares
1 onion, chopped
2 garlic cloves, crushed
2 celery sticks, chopped
50 g/1¾ oz farfalline or spaghetti, broken into small pieces
400 g/14 oz canned brown lentils, drained
1.2 litres/2 pints hot ham or vegetable stock
2 tbsp chopped fresh mint

NUTRITION
Calories 225; Sugars 1 g; Protein 13 g; Carbohydrate 27 g; Fat 8 g; Saturates 3 g

 very easy
 5 mins
5 mins
25 mins

🍴 **COOK'S TIP**
If you prefer to use dried lentils, add the stock before the pasta and cook for 1–1¼ hours, or until the lentils are tender. Add the pasta and cook for a further 12–15 minutes.

Italian cooks have created some very heart-warming soups and this is the most famous of all.

Minestrone

SERVES 4

55 g/2 oz butter
50 ml/2 fl oz olive oil
55 g/2 oz rindless fatty bacon, diced finely
3 garlic cloves, chopped finely
3 large onions, chopped finely
2 celery sticks, chopped finely
2 large carrots, chopped finely
2 large potatoes, chopped finely
100 g/3½ oz French beans, chopped finely
100 g/3½ oz courgettes, chopped finely
1.5 litres/2¾ pints vegetable or chicken stock
1 bunch fresh basil, chopped finely
100 g/3½ oz canned chopped tomatoes
2 tbsp tomato purée
100 g/3½ oz Parmesan cheese rind
85 g/3 oz dried spaghetti, broken up
salt and pepper
freshly grated Parmesan cheese, to serve

1 Heat the butter and oil together in a large saucepan, add the bacon and fry for 2 minutes. Add the garlic and onion and fry for 2 minutes, then stir in the celery, carrots and potatoes and fry for a further 2 minutes.

2 Add the beans to the pan and fry for 2 minutes. Stir in the courgettes and fry for a further 2 minutes. Cover the pan and cook all the vegetables, stirring frequently, for 15 minutes.

3 Add the stock, basil, tomatoes, tomato purée and Parmesan cheese rind and season to taste. Bring to the boil, lower the heat and simmer for 1 hour. Remove and discard the cheese rind.

4 Add the spaghetti to the pan and cook for a further 20 minutes.

5 Serve in large, warm soup bowls sprinkled with generous amounts of freshly grated Parmesan cheese.

NUTRITION
Calories 231; Sugars 3 g; Protein 8 g; Carbohydrate 14 g; Fat 16 g; Saturates 7 g

easy
10 mins
1 hr 45 mins

COOK'S TIP
You can use any variety of small pasta shapes instead of the spaghetti.

A dish with proud Mediterranean origins, this soup is a winter warmer. Serve with warm, crusty bread and, if you like, a slice of cheese.

Bean *and* Pasta Soup

1 Put the soaked beans into a large saucepan, cover with cold water and bring to the boil. Boil rapidly for 15 minutes to remove any harmful toxins. Drain the beans in a colander.

2 Heat the oil in a pan over a medium heat and fry the onions until they are just beginning to change colour. Stir in the garlic and cook for 1 further minute. Stir in the chopped tomatoes, oregano and the tomato purée and pour on the water. Add the beans, bring to the boil and cover the pan. Simmer for 45 minutes or until the beans are almost tender.

3 Add the pasta, season the soup with salt and pepper to taste and stir in the sun-dried tomatoes. Return the soup to the boil, partly cover the pan and continue cooking for 10 minutes, or until the pasta is nearly tender.

4 Stir in the coriander or parsley. Taste the soup and adjust the seasoning if necessary. Transfer to a warmed soup tureen to serve. Sprinkle with the cheese and serve hot.

SERVES 4

225 g/8 oz dried haricot beans, soaked overnight, drained and rinsed
4 tbsp olive oil
2 large onions, sliced
3 garlic cloves, chopped
400 g/14 oz canned chopped tomatoes
1 tsp dried oregano
1 tsp tomato purée
850 ml/1½ pints water
90 g/3 oz small pasta shapes, such as fusilli or conchigliette
125 g/4½ oz sun-dried tomatoes, drained and sliced thinly
1 tbsp chopped fresh coriander, or fresh flat-leaved parsley
salt and pepper
2 tbsp freshly grated Parmesan cheese, to serve

NUTRITION
Calories *463*; Sugars *5 g*; Protein *13 g*; Carbohydrate *30 g*; Fat *33 g*; Saturates *7 g*

  easy

8 hrs 10 mins

1 hr 15 mins

This soup is the traditional *Minestra* served at Easter and Christmas in the province of Parma.

Ravioli *alla* Parmigiana

SERVES 4

280 g/10 oz Basic Pasta Dough (see page 9)
1.2 litres/2 pints veal stock
freshly grated Parmesan cheese, to serve

filling
100 g/3½ oz freshly grated Parmesan cheese
100 g/3½ oz fine white breadcrumbs
2 eggs
125 ml/4 fl oz Espagnole Sauce
   (see page 15)
1 small onion, finely chopped
1 tsp freshly grated nutmeg

1 Make the Basic Pasta Dough (see page 9). Carefully roll out 2 sheets of the pasta dough and cover with a damp tea towel while you make the filling for the ravioli.

2 To make the filling, mix together the grated Parmesan cheese, fine white breadcrumbs, eggs, Espagnole Sauce (see page 15), onion and the nutmeg in a large mixing bowl.

3 Place spoonfuls of the filling at regular intervals on 1 sheet of pasta dough. Cover with the second sheet of pasta dough, then cut into squares and press the edges together to seal them.

4 Bring the veal stock to the boil in a large saucepan. Add the ravioli to the pan and cook for about 15 minutes.

5 Transfer the soup and ravioli to warm serving bowls and serve at once, generously sprinkled with freshly grated Parmesan cheese.

NUTRITION
Calories 554; Sugars 3 g; Protein 26 g;
Carbohydrate 64 g; Fat 24 g; Saturates 9 g

challenging
4 hrs 30 mins–5 hrs
25 mins

This satisfying soup makes a good lunch or supper dish and you can use any vegetables that you have to hand. Children will love the tiny pasta shapes.

Chicken *and* Pasta Soup

1 Heat the oil in a large saucepan and quickly fry the chicken and vegetables until they are lightly coloured.

2 Stir in the stock and herbs. Bring to the boil and add the pasta shapes. Return to the boil, cover and simmer for 10 minutes, stirring occasionally to prevent the pasta sticking together.

3 Season with salt and pepper to taste and serve at once, sprinkled with Parmesan cheese, if using, and fresh crusty bread.

SERVES 4

2 tbsp sunflower oil
350 g/12 oz boneless, skinless chicken breasts, diced finely
1 medium onion, diced
250 g/9 oz carrots, diced
250 g/9 oz cauliflower florets
850 ml/1½ pints chicken stock
2 tsp dried mixed herbs
125 g/4½ oz small pasta shapes
salt and pepper

to serve
Parmesan cheese, grated (optional)
crusty bread

NUTRITION
Calories *185*; Sugars *5 g*; Protein *17 g*;
Carbohydrate *20 g*; Fat *5 g*; Saturates *1 g*

        easy

          5 mins

          15–20 mins

🍲 COOK'S TIP

You can use any small pasta shapes for this soup – try conchigliette or ditalini or even spaghetti broken up into small pieces. To make a fun soup for children, try adding animal-shaped or alphabet pasta.

Veal plays an important role in Italian cuisine and there are dozens of recipes for all cuts of this meat.

Tuscan Veal Broth

SERVES 4

55 g/2 oz dried peas, soaked for 2 hours and drained
900 g/2 lb boned neck of veal, diced
1.2 litres/2 pints beef or brown stock (see page 16)
600 ml/1 pint water
55 g/2 oz barley, washed
1 large carrot, diced
1 small turnip (about 175 g/6 oz), diced
1 large leek, sliced thinly
1 red onion, chopped finely
100 g/3½ oz canned chopped tomatoes
1 fresh basil sprig
100 g/3½ oz dried vermicelli
salt and white pepper

1 Put the peas, veal, stock and water into a large saucepan and bring to the boil over a low heat. Using a slotted spoon, skim off any scum that rises to the surface of the liquid.

2 When all of the scum has been removed, add the barley and a pinch of salt to the mixture. Simmer gently over a low heat for 25 minutes.

3 Add the carrot, turnip, leek, onion, tomatoes and basil to the pan and season with salt and pepper to taste. Leave to simmer for about 2 hours, skimming the surface, using a slotted spoon, from time to time. Remove the pan from the heat and then set aside for 2 hours.

4 Set the pan over a medium heat and bring to the boil. Add the vermicelli and cook for 12 minutes. Season with salt and pepper to taste and remove and discard the basil. Ladle into soup bowls and serve immediately.

NUTRITION
Calories 420; Sugars 5 g; Protein 54 g;
Carbohydrate 37 g; Fat 7 g; Saturates 2 g

 challenging
4 hrs 15 mins
2 hrs 45 mins

 COOK'S TIP

Lentils or split peas would work equally well in this recipe. These would not need to be soaked, reducing the preparation time.

There are many varieties of fish soup in Italy, some including shellfish. This one, from Tuscany, is more like a chowder.

Fish Soup

1 Cut the fish into slices and put into a saucepan with half the onion and celery, the parsley sprigs, bay leaves, wine and water. Bring to the boil, cover and simmer for 25 minutes.

2 Strain the fish stock and discard the vegetables. Skin the fish, remove any bones and reserve the fish.

3 Heat the oil in a saucepan. Fry the remaining onion and celery with the garlic and carrot until soft, but not coloured, stirring occasionally. Add the tomatoes, potatoes, tomato purée, oregano, reserved stock and seasoning. Bring to the boil and simmer for about 15 minutes or until the potato is almost tender.

4 Meanwhile, thoroughly scrub the mussels. Add the mussels to the saucepan with the prawns and leave to simmer for about 5 minutes or until the mussels have opened (discard any that remain closed).

5 Return the reserved fish to the soup with the chopped parsley, bring back to the boil and simmer for 5 minutes. Adjust the seasoning.

6 Serve the soup in warmed bowls with chunks of fresh crusty bread, or put a toasted slice of crusty bread in the bottom of each bowl before adding the soup. If possible, remove a few half shells from the mussels before serving.

SERVES 4

1 kg/2 lb 4 oz assorted prepared fish
2 onions, sliced thinly
2 celery sticks, sliced thinly
a few fresh parsley sprigs
2 bay leaves
150 ml/5 fl oz white wine
1 litre/1 ¾ pints water
2 tbsp olive oil
1 garlic clove, crushed
1 carrot, chopped finely
400 g/14 oz canned peeled tomatoes, puréed
2 potatoes, chopped
1 tbsp tomato purée
½ tsp dried oregano
350 g/12 oz fresh mussels
175 g/6 oz peeled prawns
2 tbsp chopped fresh parsley
salt and pepper
crusty bread, to serve

NUTRITION
Calories *305*; Sugars *3 g*; Protein *47 g*;
Carbohydrate *11 g*; Fat *7 g*; Saturates *1 g*

⭐⭐⭐   moderate
     10 mins
     1 hr

Snacks *and* Starters

In Italy, starters are known as *antipasti,* which is translated as meaning 'before the main course'. *Antipasti* usually come in three categories: meat, fish and vegetables. There are many varieties of cold meats, including ham, invariably sliced paper-thin. All varieties of fish are popular in Italy, including squid, octopus, cuttlefish and fresh sardines. Seafood is also highly prized, especially huge prawns and mussels. Numerous vegetables feature in Italian cuisine and are an important part of the daily diet. They are served as a starter, as an accompaniment to main dishes, or as a course on their own. In Italy, vegetables are cooked only until *al dente* – still slightly crisp. This ensures that they retain more nutrients and the colours remain bright and appealing.

Nudo or naked is the word used to describe this mixture, which can also be made into thin pancakes or used as a filling for tortelloni.

Spinach *and* Ricotta Patties

SERVES 4

450 g/1 lb fresh spinach
250 g/9 oz ricotta cheese
1 egg, beaten
2 tsp fennel seeds, lightly crushed
50 g/1³/₄ oz pecorino or Parmesan cheese, finely grated
25 g/1 oz plain flour, mixed with 1 tsp dried thyme
75 g/2³/₄ oz butter
2 garlic cloves, crushed
salt and pepper

1 Wash the spinach and trim off any long stalks. Place in a saucepan, cover and cook for 4–5 minutes, or until wilted. This will probably have to be done in batches as the volume of spinach is quite large. Place in a colander and leave to drain and cool.

2 Mash the ricotta and beat in the egg and the fennel seeds. Season with plenty of salt and pepper, then stir in the pecorino or Parmesan cheese.

3 Squeeze as much excess water as possible from the spinach and finely chop the leaves. Stir the spinach into the cheese mixture.

4 Taking about 1 tablespoon of the spinach and cheese mixture, shape it into a ball and flatten it slightly to form a patty. Gently roll the spinach ball in the seasoned flour. Continue this process until all of the mixture has been used up.

5 Half fill a large frying pan with water and bring to the boil. Carefully add the patties and cook for 3–4 minutes, or until they rise to the surface. Remove with a slotted spoon.

6 Melt the butter in a frying pan. Add the garlic and cook for 2–3 minutes. Pour the garlic butter over the patties, season with pepper and serve at once.

NUTRITION

Calories *374*; Sugars *4 g*; Protein *16 g*;
Carbohydrate *9 g*; Fat *31 g*; Saturates *19 g*

moderate

5 mins

30 mins

Colourful marinated Mediterranean vegetables make a tasty starter. Serve with fresh bread or Tomato Toasts (see below).

Pepper Salad

1 Heat the oil in a large heavy-based frying pan. Add the onion, peppers, courgettes and garlic and fry gently for 20 minutes, stirring occasionally.

2 Add the vinegar, anchovies, olives and seasoning to taste, mix thoroughly and leave to cool.

3 Spoon the salad onto individual plates and sprinkle with the basil.

4 To make the Tomato Toasts, cut the French bread diagonally into 1-cm/½-inch slices.

5 Mix the garlic, tomato, oil and seasoning together, and spread thinly over each slice of bread.

6 Place the bread on a baking tray, drizzle with the olive oil and bake in a preheated oven, 220°C/425°F/Gas Mark 7, for 5–10 minutes until crisp. Serve the Tomato Toasts with the Pepper Salad.

SERVES 4

3 tbsp olive oil
1 onion, cut into wedges
2 red peppers, halved, deseeded and thickly sliced
2 yellow peppers, halved, deseeded and thickly sliced
2 large courgettes, sliced
2 garlic cloves, sliced
1 tbsp balsamic vinegar
50 g/1¾ oz anchovy fillets, chopped
25 g/1 oz black olives, stoned and halved
1 tbsp chopped fresh basil
salt and pepper

tomato toasts
small stick of French bread
1 garlic clove, crushed
1 tomato, peeled and chopped
2 tbsp olive oil

NUTRITION
Calories 234; Sugars 4 g; Protein 6 g; Carbohydrate 15 g; Fat 17 g; Saturates 2 g

 moderate
 5-10 mins
5-10 mins
35 mins

Thin slices of aubergine are fried in olive oil and garlic, and then topped with pesto sauce and finely sliced Mozzarella.

Aubergine Rolls

SERVES 4

2 aubergines, thinly sliced lengthways
5 tbsp olive oil
1 garlic clove, crushed
4 tbsp pesto
175 g/6 oz mozzarella, grated
fresh basil leaves, torn into pieces
salt and pepper
fresh basil leaves, to garnish

1 Sprinkle the aubergine slices liberally with salt and leave for 10–15 minutes to extract the bitter juices. Turn the slices over and repeat. Rinse well with cold water and drain on kitchen paper.

2 Heat the olive oil in a large frying pan and add the garlic and aubergine slices, a few at a time. Fry the aubergine lightly on both sides. Remove with a slotted spoon and drain them on paper towels.

3 Spread a little pesto onto one side of each of the aubergine slices. Top with the grated mozzarella and sprinkle with the torn basil leaves. Season with a little salt and pepper to taste. Roll up the slices and secure them with wooden cocktail sticks.

4 Arrange the aubergine rolls in a greased ovenproof baking dish. Place in a preheated oven, 180°C/ 350°F/Gas Mark 4, and bake for 8–10 minutes.

5 Transfer the aubergine rolls to a warmed serving plate. Scatter with fresh basil leaves and serve at once.

NUTRITION
Calories 278; Sugars 2 g; Protein 4 g; Carbohydrate 2 g; Fat 28 g; Saturates 7 g

moderate

15–20 mins

20 mins

🍲 **COOK'S TIP**

You could use sliced courgettes instead of the aubergine. They will take less time to fry.

These are delicious as a
starter or light supper dish.
You can vary the filling
with another fish
if you prefer.

Pancakes *with* Smoked Fish

1 To make the pancake batter, sift the flour and salt into a large bowl and make a well in the centre. Add the egg and, using a wooden spoon, begin to draw in the flour. Slowly add the milk and beat together to form a smooth batter. Set aside until required.

2 Place the fish in a large frying pan, add the milk and bring to the boil. Simmer for 10 minutes or until the fish begins to flake. Drain thoroughly, reserving the milk and the fish.

3 Melt the butter in a saucepan. Add the flour, mix to a paste and cook for 2–3 minutes. Remove the saucepan from the heat and add the reserved milk a little at a time, stirring to make a smooth sauce. Repeat with the fish stock. Return to the heat and bring to the boil, stirring. Stir in the Parmesan and season with salt and pepper to taste.

4 Grease a frying pan with a little of the oil. Add 2 tablespoons of the pancake batter, swirling it around the pan and cook for 2–3 minutes. Loosen the sides with a palette knife and flip over the pancake. Cook the other side for 2–3 minutes until golden; repeat to use up all the remaining batter. Stack the pancakes with sheets of baking parchment between them and keep warm in the oven.

5 Stir the flaked fish, peas and prawns into half of the sauce and use to fill each pancake. Pour over the remaining sauce, top with the Gruyère cheese and bake for 20 minutes until golden.

SERVES 4

pancakes
100 g/3½ oz flour
½ tsp salt
1 egg, beaten
300 ml/10 fl oz milk
1 tbsp oil, for frying

sauce
450 g/1 lb smoked haddock, skinned
300 ml/10 fl oz milk
40 g/1½ oz butter or margarine
40 g/1½ oz flour
300 ml/10 fl oz fish stock
75 g/2¾ oz Parmesan cheese, grated
100 g/3½ oz frozen peas, defrosted
100 g/3½ oz cooked prawns, peeled
50 g/1¾ oz Gruyère cheese, grated
salt and pepper

NUTRITION
Calories *399*; Sugars *6 g*; Protein *36 g*;
Carbohydrate *25 g*; Fat *18 g*; Saturates *10 g*

✪✪✪ moderate

🕐 15 mins

🕐 40–45 mins

These deep-fried Mozzarella sandwiches are a tasty snack at any time of the day, or serve smaller triangles as an antipasto with drinks.

Mozzarella *in* Carriages

SERVES 4

8 slices bread, preferably slightly stale, crusts removed
100 g/3½ oz mozzarella cheese, sliced thickly
50 g/1¾ oz black olives, chopped
8 canned anchovy fillets, drained and chopped
16 fresh basil leaves
4 eggs, beaten
150 ml/5 fl oz milk
oil, for deep-frying
salt and pepper

1 Cut each slice of bread into 2 triangles. Top 8 of the bread triangles with equal amounts of the mozzarella slices, olives and anchovies.

2 Place the basil leaves on top and season with salt and pepper to taste.

3 Lay the other 8 triangles of bread over the top and press down round the edges to seal.

4 Mix the eggs and milk together and pour into an ovenproof dish. Add the sandwiches and leave to soak for about 5 minutes.

5 Heat the oil in a large saucepan to 180°–190°C/350°–375°F or until a cube of bread browns in 30 seconds.

6 Before cooking the sandwiches, squeeze the edges together again.

7 Carefully place the sandwiches in the oil and deep-fry for 2 minutes or until golden, turning once. (You will have to cook them in batches.) Remove the sandwiches with a slotted spoon and drain on kitchen paper. Serve immediately while still hot.

NUTRITION
Calories *379*; Sugars *22 g*; Protein *20 g*; Carbohydrate *28 g*; Fat *22 g*; Saturates *5 g*

⭐ very easy
🕐 20 mins
🕐 5–10 mins

 COOK'S TIP

Bread that is one or two days old is much easier to handle and is much less likely to crumble.

Fennel is used extensively in northern Italy. It is a very versatile vegetable, which is good cooked or used raw in salads.

Baked Fennel

1 Using a sharp knife, trim the fennel, discarding any tough outer leaves, and cut the bulb into quarters.

2 Bring a large saucepan of water to the boil, add the fennel and celery and cook for 8–10 minutes or until just tender. Remove with a slotted spoon and leave to drain.

3 Place the fennel, celery and sun-dried tomatoes in a large ovenproof dish.

4 Mix the passata and oregano together and pour the mixture over the fennel in the dish.

5 Sprinkle with the Parmesan cheese and bake in a preheated oven at 190°C/375°F/Gas Mark 5 for 20 minutes or until hot. Serve as a starter with bread or as a vegetable side dish.

SERVES 4

2 fennel bulbs
2 celery sticks, cut into 7.5-cm/3-inch sticks
6 sun-dried tomatoes, halved
200 g/7 oz passata
2 tsp dried oregano
50 g/1¾ oz Parmesan cheese, grated

NUTRITION
Calories 111; Sugars 6 g; Protein 7 g; Carbohydrate 7 g; Fat 7 g; Saturates 3 g

 easy

 10 mins

35 mins

This quick and easy casserole can be eaten as a healthy supper dish or as a side dish to accompany sausages or grilled fish.

Casserole *of* Beans *in* Tomato Sauce

SERVES 4

400g/14 oz canned cannellini beans
400g/14 oz canned borlotti beans
2 tbsp olive oil
1 celery stick, chopped
2 garlic cloves, chopped
175 g/6 oz baby onions, halved
450 g/1 lb tomatoes
75 g/2¾ oz rocket

1 Drain the canned beans and reserve 6 tablespoons of the liquid.

2 Heat the oil in a large saucepan. Add the celery, garlic and onions and then sauté for 5 minutes, or until the onions are golden.

3 Cut a cross in the base of each tomato and plunge them into a bowl of boiling water for 30 seconds, or until the skins split. Remove them with a slotted spoon and leave until cool enough to handle. Peel off the skin and chop the flesh. Add the tomato flesh and the reserved bean liquid to the saucepan and cook for 5 minutes.

4 Add the beans to the saucepan and cook for a further 3–4 minutes, or until the beans are hot.

5 Stir in the rocket and allow to wilt slightly before serving.

NUTRITION
Calories 273; Sugars 8 g; Protein 15 g;
Carbohydrate 40 g; Fat 7 g; Saturates 1 g

moderate

10 mins

15 mins

🐞 COOK'S TIP

Another way to peel tomatoes is to cut a cross in the base, push the tomato onto a fork and hold it over a gas flame, turning it slowly so that the skin heats evenly all over. The skin will start to bubble and split, and should slide off easily.

Serve as a starter, or simply spread on small pieces of crusty fried bread (crostini) as an appetizer with drinks.

Crostini *alla* Fiorentina

1   Heat the oil in a pan, add the onion, celery, carrot and garlic, and cook gently for 4–5 minutes or until the onion is soft, but not coloured.

2   Meanwhile, rinse and dry the chicken livers. Dry the calf's liver (or other liver used), and slice into strips. Add the liver to the pan and fry gently for a few minutes until the strips are well sealed on all sides.

3   Add half of the wine and cook until it has mostly evaporated. Then add the remaining wine, tomato purée, half of the parsley, the anchovy fillets, stock or water, a little salt and plenty of pepper.

4   Cover the pan and leave to simmer, stirring occasionally, for 15–20 minutes or until tender and most of the liquid has been absorbed.

5   Leave the mixture to cool a little, then either coarsely mince or put into a food processor and process to a chunky purée.

6   Return to the pan and add the butter, capers and remaining parsley. Heat through gently until the butter melts. Adjust the seasoning and turn out into a bowl. Serve warm or cold spread on the slices of crusty bread and sprinkled with chopped parsley.

SERVES   4

3 tbsp olive oil
1 onion, chopped
1 celery stick, chopped
1 carrot, chopped
1–2 garlic cloves, crushed
125 g/4½ oz chicken livers
125 g/4½ oz calf's, lamb's or pig's liver
150 ml/5 fl oz red wine
1 tbsp tomato purée
2 tbsp chopped fresh parsley
3–4 canned anchovy fillets, chopped finely
2 tbsp stock or water
25–40 g/1–1½ oz butter
1 tbsp capers
salt and pepper
small pieces of fried crusty bread, to serve
chopped fresh parsley, to garnish

NUTRITION
Calories 393; Sugars 2 g; Protein 17 g;
Carbohydrate 19 g; Fat 25 g; Saturates 9 g

★★★   moderate
         10 mins
         40–45 mins

Deep-fried seafood is popular all around the Mediterranean, where fresh fish of all kinds is abundant. Serve with garlic mayonnaise and lemon wedges.

Crispy Golden Seafood

SERVES 4

200 g/7 oz prepared squid
200 g/7 oz blue tiger prawns, peeled
150 g/5½ oz whitebait
oil, for deep-frying
50 g/1¾ oz plain flour
1 tsp dried basil
salt and pepper

to serve
garlic mayonnaise (see Cook's Tip)
lemon wedges

1 Carefully rinse the squid, prawns and whitebait under cold running water, completely removing any accumulated dirt or grit.

2 Using a sharp knife, slice the squid into thick rings, but leave the tentacles whole.

3 Heat the oil in a large saucepan to 180°–190°C/350°–375°F, or until a cube of bread browns in 30 seconds.

4 Place the flour in a bowl and season with the salt, pepper and basil.

5 Roll the squid, prawns and whitebait in the seasoned flour until thoroughly coated all over. Carefully shake off any excess flour.

6 Cook the seafood in the heated oil in batches for 2–3 minutes, or until crispy and golden all over. Remove each batch of the seafood with a slotted spoon and then leave to drain thoroughly on kitchen paper.

7 Transfer the deep-fried seafood to serving plates and then serve with garlic mayonnaise (see Cook's Tip) and lemon wedges.

NUTRITION
Calories *393*; Sugars *0.2 g*; Protein *27 g*;
Carbohydrate *12 g*; Fat *26 g*; Saturates *3 g*

easy
5 mins
15 mins

 COOK'S TIP

To make garlic mayonnaise for serving with the deep-fried seafood, crush 2 garlic cloves, stir into 8 tablespoons of mayonnaise, season with salt and pepper and add a little chopped fresh parsley.

Simple and quick to make, this spicy dish is sure to set the taste buds tingling.

Chorizo *and* Wild Mushrooms

1   Bring a large saucepan of lightly salted water to the boil. Add the vermicelli and 1 tablespoon of the oil and cook for 8–10 minutes or until just tender, but still firm to the bite.

2   Drain the pasta thoroughly, place on a large, warm serving plate and keep warm until needed.

3   Meanwhile, heat the remaining oil in a large frying pan. Add the garlic and fry for 1 minute.

4   Add the chorizo and wild mushrooms and cook for 4 minutes. Add the chopped chillies and cook for a further minute.

5   Pour the chorizo and wild mushroom mixture over the vermicelli and season with a little salt and pepper.

6   Sprinkle with freshly grated Parmesan cheese, garnish with a lattice of anchovy fillets and serve immediately.

SERVES 4

680 g/1½ lb dried vermicelli
125 ml/4 fl oz olive oil
2 garlic cloves
125 g/4½ oz chorizo, sliced
225 g/8 oz wild mushrooms
3 fresh red chillies, chopped
2 tbsp freshly grated Parmesan cheese
salt and pepper
10 anchovy fillets, to garnish

NUTRITION
Calories *495*; Sugars *1 g*; Protein *15 g*; Carbohydrate *33 g*; Fat *35 g*; Saturates *5 g*

easy

5 mins

20 mins

 COOK'S TIP

Many varieties of mushrooms are available, most indistinguishable from the wild varieties. Mixed colour oyster mushrooms are used here, but you could try chanterelles. Chanterelles shrink during cooking, so you may need more.

Served with freshly made Italian bread or tossed with pesto, this makes a mouthwatering light lunch.

Smoked Ham Linguine

SERVES 4

450 g/1 lb dried linguine
450 g/1 lb broccoli florets
150 ml/5 fl oz Cheese Sauce (see page 15)
225 g/8 oz Italian smoked ham
salt and pepper
Italian bread, to serve

1 Bring a large pan of lightly salted water to the boil. Add the linguine and broccoli florets and cook for 10 minutes, or until the linguine is tender, but still firm to the bite.

2 Drain the linguine and broccoli thoroughly, then set aside and keep warm.

3 Meanwhile, make the Cheese Sauce.

4 Cut the Italian smoked ham into thin strips. Toss the linguine, broccoli and ham into the Cheese Sauce, and then gently warm through over a very low heat. Do not overheat.

5 Transfer the pasta mixture to a warm serving dish. Sprinkle with black pepper and serve with Italian bread.

NUTRITION
Calories 537; Sugars 4 g; Protein 22 g; Carbohydrate 71 g; Fat 29 g; Saturates 8 g

moderate

25 mins

15 mins

🍽 COOK'S TIP

There are many types of Italian bread which would be suitable to serve with this dish. Ciabatta is made with olive oil and is available plain and with different ingredients, such as olives or sun-dried tomatoes.

Prepare the marinated aubergines well in advance so that all you have to do is cook the pasta.

Aubergine *on a* Bed *of* Linguine

1 Put the vegetable stock, wine vinegar and balsamic vinegar into a saucepan and bring to the boil over a low heat. Add 2 teaspoons of the olive oil and the sprig of oregano and simmer gently for about 1 minute.

2 Add the aubergine slices to the pan, remove from the heat and set aside for 10 minutes.

3 Meanwhile make the marinade. Combine the oil, garlic, fresh oregano, almonds, pepper, lime juice, orange rind and juice together in a large bowl and season to taste.

4 Carefully remove the aubergine from the saucepan with a slotted spoon, and drain well. Add the aubergine slices to the marinade, mixing well, and set aside in the refrigerator for about 12 hours.

5 Bring a large pan of lightly salted water to the boil. Add half of the remaining oil and the linguine and cook for 8–10 minutes until just tender. Drain the pasta thoroughly and toss with the remaining oil while still warm. Arrange the pasta on a serving plate with the aubergine slices and the marinade and serve.

S E R V E S   4

150 ml/5 fl oz vegetable stock
150 ml/5 fl oz white wine vinegar
2 tsp balsamic vinegar
3 tbsp olive oil
fresh oregano sprig
450 g/1 lb aubergine, peeled and
    sliced thinly
400 g/14 oz dried linguine

marinade
2 tbsp extra-virgin olive oil
2 garlic cloves, crushed
2 tbsp chopped fresh oregano
2 tbsp finely chopped roasted almonds
2 tbsp diced red pepper
2 tbsp lime juice
grated rind and juice of 1 orange
salt and pepper

N U T R I T I O N
Calories *378*; Sugars *3 g*; Protein *12 g*;
Carbohydrate *16 g*; Fat *30 g*; Saturates *3 g*

 challenging

 12 hrs 15 mins

15 mins

This is a classic combination in which the smooth, creamy cheese balances the stronger taste of the spinach.

Spinach *and* Ricotta Shells

SERVES 4

400 g/14 oz dried lumache rigate grande
5 tbsp olive oil
55 g/2 oz fresh white breadcrumbs
125 ml/4 fl oz milk
300 g/10½ oz frozen spinach, thawed and drained
225 g/8 oz ricotta cheese
pinch of freshly grated nutmeg
400 g/14 oz canned chopped tomatoes, drained
1 garlic clove, crushed
salt and pepper

1 Bring a large saucepan of lightly salted water to the boil. Add the lumache and 1 tablespoon of the olive oil and cook for 8–10 minutes until just tender, but still firm to the bite. Drain the pasta, refresh under cold water and set aside until required.

2 Put the breadcrumbs, milk and 3 tablespoons of the remaining olive oil in a food processor and work to combine.

3 Add the spinach and ricotta cheese to the food processor and work to a smooth mixture. Transfer to a bowl, stir in the nutmeg, and season with salt and pepper to taste.

4 Mix together the tomatoes, garlic and remaining oil and spoon the mixture into the base of a large ovenproof dish.

5 Using a teaspoon, fill the lumache with the spinach and ricotta mixture and arrange on top of the tomato mixture in the dish. Cover and bake in a preheated oven at 180°C/350°F/Gas 4 for 20 minutes. Serve hot.

NUTRITION
Calories *673*; Sugars *10 g*; Protein *23 g*; Carbohydrate *93 g*; Fat *26 g*; Saturates *8 g*

moderate
10 mins
30 mins

🍲 **COOK'S TIP**

Ricotta is a creamy Italian cheese traditionally made from ewe's milk whey. It is soft and white, with a smooth texture and a slightly sweet flavour. It should be used within 2–3 days of purchase.

This colourful light meal can be made with a variety of different pasta, including spaghetti and linguine.

Fettuccine *with* Anchovy *and* Spinach

1 Trim off any tough spinach stalks. Rinse the spinach leaves and place them in a large saucepan with only the water that is clinging to them after washing. Cover and cook over a high heat, shaking the saucepan from time to time, until the spinach has wilted, but retains its colour. Drain well, set aside and keep warm.

2 Bring a large saucepan of lightly salted water to the boil. Add the fettuccine and 1 tablespoon of the oil and cook for 8–10 minutes until it is just tender, but still firm to the bite.

3 Heat 4 tablespoons of the remaining oil in a saucepan. Add the pine kernels and fry until golden. Remove the pine kernels from the pan and set aside until required.

4 Add the garlic to the pan and fry until golden. Add the anchovies and stir in the spinach. Cook, stirring, for 2–3 minutes, until heated through. Return the pine kernels to the pan.

5 Drain the fettuccine, toss in the remaining olive oil and transfer to a warm serving dish. Spoon the anchovy and spinach sauce over the fettuccine, toss lightly and serve immediately.

COOK'S TIP

If you are in a hurry, you can use frozen spinach. Thaw and drain it thoroughly, pressing out as much moisture as possible. Cut the leaves into strips and add to the dish with the anchovies in step 4.

SERVES 4

900 g/2 lb fresh young spinach leaves
400 g/14 oz dried fettuccine
6 tbsp olive oil
3 tbsp pine kernels
3 garlic cloves, crushed
8 canned anchovy fillets, drained
    and chopped
salt

NUTRITION
Calories *619*; Sugars *5 g*; Protein *21 g*;
Carbohydrate *67 g*; Fat *31 g*; Saturates *3 g*

        easy

        10 mins

        25 mins

This simple, creamy pasta sauce is a classic Italian recipe.

Tagliarini *with* Gorgonzola

SERVES 4

25 g/1 oz butter
225 g/8 oz Gorgonzola cheese, roughly crumbled
150 ml/5 fl oz double cream
30 ml/1 fl oz dry white wine
1 tsp cornflour
4 fresh sage sprigs, finely chopped
400 g/14 oz dried tagliarini
2 tbsp olive oil
salt and white pepper

1 Melt the butter in a heavy-based saucepan. Stir in 175 g/6 oz of the Gorgonzola cheese and melt, over a low heat, for about 2 minutes.

2 Add the cream, wine and cornflour and beat with a whisk until fully incorporated.

3 Stir in the sage and season to taste with salt and white pepper. Bring to the boil over a low heat, whisking constantly, until the sauce thickens. Remove from the heat and set aside while you cook the pasta.

4 Bring a large saucepan of lightly salted water to the boil. Add the tagliarini and 1 tbsp of the olive oil. Cook the pasta for 12–14 minutes, or until just tender, then drain thoroughly and toss in the remaining olive oil. Transfer the pasta to a serving dish and keep warm.

5 Return the saucepan containing the sauce to a low heat to reheat the sauce, whisking constantly. Spoon the Gorgonzola sauce over the tagliarini, generously sprinkle over the remaining cheese and serve immediately.

NUTRITION

Calories *904*; Sugars *4 g*; Protein *27 g*;
Carbohydrate *83 g*; Fat *53 g*; Saturates *36 g*

easy
5 mins
20 mins

🍴 COOK'S TIP

Gorgonzola is one of the world's oldest veined cheeses. When buying, check that it is creamy yellow with delicate green veining. Avoid hard or discoloured cheese. It should have a rich, piquant aroma, not a bitter smell.

This light pasta dish has a delicate flavour ideally suited to a summer lunch.

Spaghetti *with* Ricotta Cheese

1 Bring a large pan of lightly salted water to the boil. Add the spaghetti and 1 tablespoon of the oil and cook until tender, but still firm to the bite.

2 Drain the pasta, return to the pan and toss with the butter and chopped parsley. Set aside and keep warm.

3 To make the sauce, mix together the ground almonds, ricotta cheese, nutmeg, cinnamon and crème fraîche in a saucepan over a low heat to form a thick paste. Gradually stir in the remaining oil. When the oil has been fully incorporated, gradually stir in the hot chicken stock, until smooth. Season to taste with pepper.

4 Transfer the spaghetti to a warm serving dish, pour over the sauce and toss together well (see Cook's Tip). Sprinkle over the pine nuts, garnish with the flat-leaved parsley and serve warm.

SERVES 4

350 g/12 oz dried spaghetti
3 tbsp olive oil
40 g/1½ oz butter
2 tbsp chopped fresh flat-leaved parsley
125 g/4½ oz freshly ground almonds
125 g/4½ oz ricotta cheese
pinch of freshly grated nutmeg
pinch of ground cinnamon
150 ml/5 fl oz crème fraîche
125 ml/4 fl oz hot chicken stock
1 tbsp pine kernels
salt and pepper
fresh flat-leaved parsley sprigs, to garnish

NUTRITION

Calories 701; Sugars 12 g; Protein 17 g; Carbohydrate 73 g; Fat 40 g; Saturates 15 g

 easy

 5 mins

25 mins

COOK'S TIP

Use two large forks to toss spaghetti or other long pasta, so that it is thoroughly coated with the sauce. Special spaghetti forks are available from some cookware departments and kitchen shops.

This is quick and simple, but one of the nicest of Italian fried fish dishes, served with penne.

Penne *with* Fried Mussels

SERVES 4
400 g/14 oz dried penne
125 ml/4 fl oz olive oil
450 g/1 lb mussels, cooked and shelled
1 tsp sea salt
90 g/3 oz flour
100 g/3½ oz sun-dried tomatoes, sliced
2 tbsp chopped fresh basil leaves
salt and pepper
1 lemon, sliced thinly, to garnish

1 Bring a large saucepan of lightly salted water to the boil. Add the penne and 1 tbsp of the olive oil and cook for 8–10 minutes or until the pasta is just tender, but still firm to the bite.

2 Drain the pasta thoroughly and place in a large, warm serving dish. Set aside and keep warm while you cook the mussels.

3 Lightly sprinkle the mussels with the sea salt. Season the flour with salt and pepper to taste, sprinkle into a bowl and toss the mussels in the flour until well coated.

4 Heat the remaining oil in a large frying pan. Add the mussels and fry, stirring frequently, until a golden brown colour.

5 Toss the mussels with the penne and sprinkle with the sun-dried tomatoes and basil leaves. Garnish with slices of lemon and serve immediately.

NUTRITION
Calories 537; Sugars 2 g; Protein 22 g;
Carbohydrate 62 g; Fat 24 g; Saturates 3 g

easy
10 mins
25 mins

 COOK'S TIP

Sun-dried tomatoes, used in Italy for a long time, have become popular elsewhere only recently. They are dried and then preserved in oil. They have a concentrated, roasted flavour and a dense texture.

Ribbed tubes of pasta are filled with tuna and ricotta cheese and then baked in a creamy sauce.

Baked Tuna *and* Ricotta Rigatoni

1 Lightly grease a large ovenproof dish with butter.

2 Bring a large saucepan of lightly salted water to the boil. Add the rigatoni and olive oil and cook for 8–10 minutes until just tender, but still firm to the bite. Drain the pasta and set aside until cool enough to handle.

3 Meanwhile, in a bowl, mix together the tuna and ricotta cheese to form a soft paste. Spoon the mixture into a piping bag and use to fill the rigatoni. Arrange the filled pasta tubes side by side in the prepared ovenproof dish.

4 To make the sauce, mix the cream and Parmesan cheese together in a bowl and season with salt and pepper to taste. Spoon the sauce over the rigatoni and top with the sun-dried tomatoes, arranged in a criss-cross pattern. Bake in a preheated oven, at 200°C/400°F/Gas Mark 6, for 20 minutes. Serve hot straight from the dish.

SERVES 4

butter, for greasing
450 g/1 lb dried rigatoni
1 tbsp olive oil
200 g/7 oz canned, flaked tuna, drained
225 g/8 oz ricotta cheese
125 ml/4 fl oz double cream
225 g/8 oz grated Parmesan cheese
125 g/4 oz sun-dried tomatoes, drained and sliced
salt and pepper

NUTRITION
Calories 949; Sugars 5 g; Protein 51 g; Carbohydrate 85 g; Fat 48 g; Saturates 26 g

 moderate

15 mins

30 mins

 COOK'S TIP

For a vegetarian alternative of this recipe, simply substitute a mixture of stoned and chopped black olives and chopped walnuts for the tuna. Follow exactly the same cooking method.

This filling vegetarian
dish is perfect for an
inexpensive and
quick lunch.

Rotelle *with* Spicy Italian Sauce

SERVES 4

5 tbsp olive oil
3 garlic cloves, crushed
2 fresh red chillies, chopped
1 fresh green chilli, chopped
200 ml/7 fl oz Italian Red Wine Sauce
   (see page 15)
400 g/14 oz dried rotelle
salt and pepper
warm Italian bread, to serve

1 Heat 4 tablespoons of the oil in a saucepan. Add the garlic and chillies and fry for 3 minutes.

2 Stir in the Italian Red Wine Sauce, season with salt and pepper to taste and simmer gently over a low heat for 20 minutes.

3 Bring a large saucepan of lightly salted water to the boil. Add the rotelle and the remaining oil and cook for 8 minutes, until just tender, but still firm to the bite. Drain the pasta.

4 Toss the rotelle in the spicy sauce, transfer to a warm serving dish and serve with warm Italian bread.

NUTRITION

Calories *530*; Sugars *4 g*; Protein *13 g*;
Carbohydrate *78 g*; Fat *18 g*; Saturates *3 g*

moderate
10 mins
1 hr

 COOK'S TIP

Handle chillies as little as possible – wear rubber gloves if necessary. Always wash your hands well. Don't touch your face or eyes before washing your hands. Remove the seeds before chopping chillies; they are the hottest part.

Deliciously sweet roasted tomatoes are filled with home-made lemon mayonnaise and tuna.

Tuna-Stuffed Tomatoes

1 Halve the tomatoes and scoop out the seeds. Divide the sun-dried tomato purée among the tomato halves and spread around the inside of the skin.

2 Place on a baking tray and roast in a preheated oven at 200°C/400°F/Gas Mark 6 for 12–15 minutes. Leave to cool slightly.

3 Meanwhile, make the mayonnaise. In a food processor, blend the egg yolks and lemon juice with the lemon rind, until smooth. Once mixed and with the motor still running slowly, add the olive oil. Stop the processor as soon as the mayonnaise has thickened. Alternatively, use a hand whisk, beating the mixture continuously until it thickens.

4 Add the tuna and capers to the mayonnaise and season.

5 Spoon the tuna mayonnaise mixture into the tomato shells and garnish with sun-dried tomato strips and basil leaves. Return to the oven for a few minutes or serve chilled.

SERVES 4

4 plum tomatoes
2 tbsp sun-dried tomato purée
2 egg yolks
2 tsp lemon juice
finely grated rind of 1 lemon
4 tbsp olive oil
115 g/4 oz canned tuna, drained
2 tbsp capers, rinsed
salt and pepper

to garnish
2 sun-dried tomatoes, cut into strips
fresh basil leaves

NUTRITION
Calories *196*; Sugars *2 g*; Protein *9 g*;
Carbohydrate *2 g*; Fat *17 g*; Saturates *3 g*

 easy

 5–10 mins

 25 mins

Fish *and* Seafood

Italians eat everything that comes out of the sea, from the tiny whitebait to the massive tuna fish. Fish markets in Italy are fascinating, with a huge variety of fish on display, but as most of the fish comes from the Mediterranean it is not always easy to find an equivalent elsewhere. However, fresh or frozen imported fish of all kinds is increasingly appearing in fishmongers and supermarkets. After pasta, fish is probably the most important source of food in Italy, and in many recipes fish or seafood are served with one type of pasta or another – a winning combination!

Sea bass is a delicious
white-fleshed fish.
If cooking two small fish,
they can be grilled; if
cooking one large fish,
bake it in the oven.

bo

Baked Sea Bass

SERVES 4

1.4 kg/3 lb fresh sea bass or 2 sea bass about
750 g/1 lb 10 oz each, gutted
2–4 fresh rosemary sprigs
½ lemon, sliced thinly
2 tbsp olive oil

garlic sauce
2 tsp coarse sea salt
2 tsp capers
2 garlic cloves, crushed
4 tbsp water
2 fresh bay leaves
1 tsp lemon juice or white wine vinegar
2 tbsp olive oil
pepper

to garnish
bay leaves
lemon wedges

NUTRITION
Calories *378*; Sugars *0 g*; Protein *62 g*;
Carbohydrate *0 g*; Fat *14 g*; Saturates *2 g*

 challenging
15–20 mins
20–55 mins

1 Descale the fish and cut off the sharp fins. Make diagonal cuts along both
sides. Wash and dry thoroughly. Place a sprig of rosemary in the cavity of
each of the smaller fish with half the lemon slices; or two sprigs and all the
lemon in the large fish.

2 To grill: place in a foil-lined pan, brush with 1–2 tbsp oil and grill under a
moderate heat for 5 minutes each side or until cooked through.

3 To bake: place the fish in a foil-lined dish or roasting tin brushed with oil,
and brush the fish with the rest of the oil. Cook in a preheated oven,
190°C/375°F/ Gas Mark 5, for 30 minutes for the small fish or 45–50 minutes
for the large fish, until the thickest part of the fish is opaque.

4 To make the sauce, crush the salt and capers with the garlic in a pestle and
mortar and then work in the water. Or, work in a food processor or blender
until smooth.

5 Bruise the bay leaves and remaining sprigs of rosemary and put in a bowl.
Add the garlic mixture, lemon juice and oil and pound together until the
flavours are released. Season with pepper to taste.

6 Place the fish on a serving dish and, if liked, remove the skin. Spoon some of
the sauce over the fish and serve the rest of the sauce separately. Garnish
with fresh bay leaves and lemon wedges.

A rich wine and cream sauce makes this an excellent dinner party dish. You can make the stock the day before so it takes only minutes to cook.

Sole Fillets *in* Marsala *and* Cream

1 To make the stock, place the water, fish bones and skin, onion, carrot and bay leaves in a saucepan and bring to the boil.

2 Reduce the heat and leave the mixture to simmer for 1 hour, or until the stock has reduced to about 150 ml/ 5 fl oz. Drain the stock through a fine sieve, discarding the bones and vegetables, and set aside.

3 To make the sauce, heat the oil and butter in a frying pan. Add the shallots and cook, stirring, for 2–3 minutes, or until just softened.

4 Add the mushrooms to the frying pan and cook, stirring, for a further 2–3 minutes, or until they are just beginning to brown.

5 Add the peppercorns and sole fillets to the frying pan. Fry the sole fillets for 3–4 minutes on each side, or until golden brown.

6 Pour the Marsala and stock over the fish and leave to simmer for 3 minutes. Remove the fish from the pan with a fish slice or a slotted spoon, set aside and keep warm.

7 Increase the heat and boil the mixture in the pan for about 5 minutes or until the sauce has reduced and thickened.

8 Pour in the cream, then return the fish to the pan and heat through. Serve with cooked vegetables of your choice.

SERVES **4**

stock
600 ml/1 pint water
bones and skin from the sole fillets
1 onion, halved
1 carrot, peeled and halved
3 fresh bay leaves

sauce
1 tbsp olive oil
15 g/½ oz butter
4 shallots, finely chopped
100 g/3½ oz baby button mushrooms, wiped and halved
1 tbsp peppercorns, lightly crushed
8 sole fillets
100 ml/3½ fl oz Marsala
150 ml/5 fl oz double cream

to serve
cooked mangetouts, carrots or other vegetables of your choice

NUTRITION
Calories 474; Sugars 3 g; Protein 47 g; Carbohydrate 3 g; Fat 28 g; Saturates 14 g

✪✪✪✪ challenging
🕐 15 mins
🕐 1 hr 30 mins

A delicious stuffing of sun-dried tomatoes and fresh lemon thyme are used to stuff whole sole.

Grilled Stuffed Sole

SERVES 4

1 tbsp olive oil
25 g/1 oz butter
1 small onion, chopped finely
1 garlic clove, chopped
3 sun-dried tomatoes, chopped
2 tbsp lemon thyme
50 g/1¾ oz breadcrumbs
1 tbsp lemon juice
4 small whole sole, gutted and cleaned
salt and pepper
lemon wedges, to garnish
fresh green salad leaves, to serve

1 Heat the oil and butter in a frying pan until it just begins to froth.

2 Add the onion and garlic to the frying pan and cook, stirring, for 5 minutes, or until just softened.

3 To make the stuffing, mix together the tomatoes, thyme, breadcrumbs, and lemon juice in a bowl, then season to taste.

4 Add the stuffing mixture to the pan, and stir to mix.

5 Using a sharp knife, pare the skin from the bone inside the gut hole of the fish to make a pocket. Spoon the tomato and herb stuffing into the pocket.

6 Cook the fish, under a preheated grill, for 6 minutes on each side, or until golden brown.

7 Transfer the stuffed fish to serving plates and garnish with lemon wedges. Serve with fresh green salad leaves.

NUTRITION
Calories *207*; Sugars *0.2 g*; Protein *24 g*;
Carbohydrate *8 g*; Fat *10 g*; Saturates *4 g*

moderate

20 mins

15 mins

 COOK'S TIP

Lemon thyme has a delicate lemon scent and flavour. Ordinary thyme can be used instead, but mix it with 1 teaspoon of lemon rind for extra flavour.

This delicate-tasting dish is surprisingly satisfying for even the largest appetites. Prepare the Italian Red Wine Sauce well in advance.

Lemon Sole *and* Haddock Ravioli

1 Flake the lemon sole and haddock fillets with a fork and transfer the flesh to a large mixing bowl.

2 Mix the eggs, cooked potato gnocchi, breadcrumbs and cream in a bowl until thoroughly combined. Add the fish to the bowl containing the gnocchi and season the mixture with salt and pepper to taste.

3 Roll out the pasta dough on to a lightly floured surface and cut out 7.5 cm/ 3 inch rounds using a plain cutter.

4 Place a spoonful of the fish stuffing on each round. Dampen the edges slightly and fold the pasta rounds over, pressing together to seal.

5 Bring a large saucepan of lightly salted water to the boil. Add the ravioli and cook for 15 minutes. Meanwhile, warm through the Italian Red Wine Sauce.

6 Drain the ravioli, using a slotted spoon, and transfer to a large serving dish. Pour over the Italian Red Wine Sauce, sprinkle over the Parmesan cheese and serve immediately.

SERVES 4

450 g/1 lb lemon sole fillets, skinned
450 g/1 lb haddock fillets, skinned
3 eggs beaten
450 g/1 lb cooked potato gnocchi
175 g/6 oz fresh breadcrumbs
50 ml/2 fl oz double cream
450 g/1 lb Basic Pasta Dough (see page 9)
300 ml/10 fl oz Italian Red Wine Sauce (see page 15)
60 g/2 oz freshly grated Parmesan cheese
salt and pepper

NUTRITION
Calories 977; Sugars 7 g; Protein 67 g; Carbohydrate 93 g; Fat 40 g; Saturates 17 g

 challenging
1 hr 40 mins
15 mins

This recipe from Trentino is best when the fish are freshly caught, but it is a good way to cook any trout, giving it an interesting flavour.

Trout *in* Red Wine

SERVES 4

4 fresh trout, about 300 g/10 oz each
250 ml/9 fl oz red or white wine vinegar
300 ml/10 fl oz red or dry white wine
150 ml/5 fl oz water
1 carrot, sliced
2–4 bay leaves
thinly pared rind of 1 lemon
1 small onion, sliced very thinly
4 fresh parsley sprigs
4 fresh thyme sprigs
1 tsp black peppercorns
6–8 whole cloves
90 g/3 oz butter
1 tbsp chopped fresh mixed herbs
salt and pepper

to garnish
fresh parsley
lemon slices

NUTRITION
Calories *489*; Sugars *0.6 g*; Protein *48 g*;
Carbohydrate *0.6 g*; Fat *27 g*; Saturates *14 g*

challenging

30 mins

45 mins

1 Gut the trout, but leave their heads on. Dry on kitchen paper and lay the fish head to tail in a shallow container or baking tin large enough to hold them.

2 Bring the wine vinegar to the boil and pour slowly all over the fish. Leave the fish to marinate in the refrigerator for about 20 minutes.

3 Meanwhile, put the wine, water, carrot, bay leaves, lemon rind, onion, herbs, peppercorns and cloves into a saucepan with a good pinch of sea salt and heat gently.

4 Drain the fish thoroughly, discarding the vinegar. Place the fish in a fish kettle or large frying pan so they touch. When the wine mixture boils, strain gently over the fish so they are about half covered. Cover the pan and simmer very gently for 15 minutes.

5 Carefully remove the fish from the tin, draining off and reserving as much of the liquid as possible. Arrange the fish on a serving dish and keep warm.

6 Boil the cooking liquid until reduced to about 4–6 tbsp. Melt the butter in a pan and strain in the cooking liquor. Season and spoon the sauce over the fish. Garnish with fresh parsley and lemon slices.

Red mullet has a beautiful pink skin, which is enhanced in this dish by being cooked in red wine.

Sardinian Red Mullet

1 Place the sultanas in a bowl. Pour over the red wine and leave to soak for 10 minutes.

2 Heat the oil in a large frying pan. Add the onions and sauté for 2 minutes.

3 Add the courgettes to the pan and fry for a further 3 minutes, or until they are tender.

4 Using a zester, pare long, thin strips from one of the oranges. Using a sharp knife, remove the skin from both of the oranges, then segment the oranges by slicing between the lines of pith.

5 Add the orange zest to the frying pan. Add the red wine, sultanas, red mullet and anchovies to the pan and leave to simmer for 10–15 minutes, or until the fish is cooked through.

6 Stir in the oregano and orange segments, set aside and leave to cool. Place the mixture in a large bowl and leave to chill, covered, in the refrigerator for at least 2 hours to allow the flavours to mingle. Transfer to serving plates and serve.

SERVES 4

50 g/1³/₄ oz sultanas
150 ml/5 fl oz red wine
2 tbsp olive oil
2 medium onions, sliced
1 courgette cut into 5-cm/2-inch sticks
2 oranges
4 red mullet, boned and filleted
50g/1³/₄ oz canned anchovy fillets, drained
2 tbsp chopped fresh oregano

 COOK'S TIP

Soaking the sultanas in the red wine gives them an incredible flavour and succulence as they soak up all the wine.

NUTRITION
Calories 287; Sugars 15 g; Protein 31 g; Carbohydrate 15 g; Fat 9 g; Saturates 1 g

✪✪✪ moderate
        2 hrs 30 mins
        25 mins

Fresh salmon and pasta in
a mouthwatering lemon
and watercress sauce –
a wonderful summer
evening treat.

Salmon Steaks *with* Penne

SERVES 4

4 x 280 g/10 oz fresh salmon steaks
55 g/2 oz butter
175 ml/6 fl oz dry white wine
sea salt
8 peppercorns
fresh dill sprig
fresh tarragon sprig
1 lemon, sliced
450 g/1 lb dried penne
2 tbsp olive oil

to garnish
lemon slices
fresh watercress

lemon & watercress sauce
25 g/1 oz butter
25 g/1 oz plain flour
150 ml/5 fl oz warm milk
juice and finely grated rind of 2 lemons
55 g/2 oz watercress, chopped
salt and pepper

NUTRITION
Calories 968; Sugars 3 g; Protein 59 g;
Carbohydrate 49 g; Fat 58 g; Saturates 19 g

easy

10 mins

40 mins

1 Put the salmon in a large, non-stick pan. Add the butter, wine, a pinch of sea salt, the peppercorns, dill, tarragon and lemon. Cover, bring to the boil, then lower the heat and simmer for 10 minutes.

2 Using a fish slice, carefully remove the salmon. Strain and reserve the cooking liquid. Remove and discard the salmon skin and centre bones. Place on a warm dish, cover and keep warm.

3 Meanwhile, bring a saucepan of salted water to the boil. Add the penne and 1 tbsp of the oil and cook for 12 minutes, or until tender, but still firm to the bite. Drain and sprinkle over the remaining olive oil. Place on a warm serving dish, top with the salmon steaks and keep warm.

4 To make the sauce, melt the butter and stir in the flour for 2 minutes. Stir in the milk and about 7 tablespoons of the reserved cooking liquid. Add the lemon juice and rind and cook, stirring, for a further 10 minutes.

5 Add the watercress to the sauce, stir gently and season to taste with salt and pepper.

6 Pour the sauce over the salmon and penne, garnish with slices of lemon and fresh watercress and serve immediately.

Fresh tuna will be either a small bonito fish or steaks from a skipjack. The more delicately flavoured fish have a paler flesh.

Tuna *with* Roast Peppers

1 Put the tuna steaks into a large bowl with the lemon juice and water. Leave for 15 minutes.

2 Drain and brush the tuna steaks all over with olive oil and season well with salt and pepper.

3 Put the peppers over a hot barbecue or under a hot grill and cook for 12 minutes until they are charred all over. Put them into a plastic bag and seal it.

4 Meanwhile, cook the tuna over a hot barbecue or under a hot grill and cook for 12–15 minutes, turning once.

5 When the peppers are cool enough to handle, peel them and cut each half into 4 strips. Toss the pepper pieces with the remaining olive oil, olives and balsamic vinegar.

6 Serve the tuna steaks piping hot, with the roasted pepper salad.

SERVES **4**

4 tuna steaks, about 250 g/9 oz each
3 tbsp lemon juice
1 litre/1³⁄₄ pints water
6 tbsp olive oil
2 orange peppers, halved and deseeded
2 red peppers, halved and deseeded
12 black olives
1 tsp balsamic vinegar
salt and pepper

NUTRITION
Calories *428*; Sugars *5 g*; Protein *60 g*;
Carbohydrate *5 g*; Fat *19 g*; Saturates *3 g*

  moderate

20 mins

30 mins

 COOK'S TIP

Red, orange and yellow peppers can be peeled by cooking them in a hot oven for 30 minutes, turning frequently, or roasting straight over a naked gas flame, again turning frequently. In both methods, deseed the peppers after peeling.

You can substitute other whole fish for the snapper, or use cutlets of cod or halibut.

Baked Red Snapper

SERVES 4

juice of 2 limes, or 1 lemon
1 red snapper, about 1.25 kg/2 lb 12 oz, cleaned
4–5 fresh thyme sprigs
3 tbsp olive oil
1 large onion, chopped
2 garlic cloves, finely chopped
400 g/14 oz canned chopped tomatoes
2 tbsp tomato purée
2 tbsp red wine vinegar
5 tbsp low-fat yogurt
2 tbsp chopped fresh parsley
2 tsp dried oregano
6 tbsp dry breadcrumbs
60 g/2 oz low-fat yogurt cheese, crumbled
salt and pepper

to garnish
lime wedges
fresh dill sprigs

1 Sprinkle the lime or lemon juice inside and over the fish and season. Place the thyme inside the fish.

2 Heat the oil in a pan and fry the onion until translucent. Stir in the garlic and cook for 1 minute, then add the tomatoes, tomato purée and vinegar. Simmer, uncovered, for 5 minutes. Allow the sauce to cool, then stir in the yogurt, parsley and oregano.

3 Pour half the sauce into an ovenproof dish just large enough for the fish. Add the fish, pour the remainder of the sauce over it, and sprinkle with breadcrumbs. Bake uncovered for 30–35 minutes. Sprinkle the cheese over the fish and serve with lime wedges and dill sprigs.

NUTRITION
Calories 519; Sugars 12 g; Protein 61 g;
Fat 23 g; Carbohydrate 18 g; Saturates 3 g

moderate

20 mins

50 mins

Marinating fish, for even a short time, adds a subtle flavour to the flesh and makes even simply grilled or fried fish delicious.

Marinated Fish

1 Using a sharp knife, cut 4 or 5 diagonal slashes on each side of the fish. Place the fish in a shallow, non-metallic dish.

2 To make the marinade, mix together the marjoram, olive oil, lime rind and juice, garlic and salt and pepper in a bowl.

3 Pour the mixture over the fish. Leave to marinate in the refrigerator for about 30 minutes.

4 Cook the mackerel, under a preheated grill, for 5–6 minutes on each side, brushing occasionally with the reserved marinade, until golden.

5 Transfer the fish to serving plates. Pour over any remaining marinade before serving, garnished with lime wedges and salad leaves.

S E R V E S 4

4 whole mackerel, cleaned and gutted
4 tbsp chopped fresh marjoram
2 tbsp extra virgin olive oil
finely grated rind and juice of 1 lime
2 garlic cloves, crushed
salt and pepper
lime wedges, to garnish
green salad leaves, to serve

N U T R I T I O N
Calories 361; Sugars 0 g; Protein 26 g;
Carbohydrate 0 g; Fat 29 g; Saturates 5 g

 moderate

45 mins

 15 mins

🍳 **C O O K ' S T I P**

If the lime is too hard to squeeze, microwave on HIGH power for 30 seconds to release the juice. This dish is also excellent cooked on the barbecue.

This adaptation of an eighteenth-century Italian dish is baked until it is golden brown and sizzling, then cut into wedges like a cake.

Macaroni *and* Prawn Bake

SERVES 4

350 g/12 oz dried short-cut macaroni
1 tbsp olive oil, plus extra for brushing
85 g/3 oz butter, plus extra for greasing
2 small fennel bulbs, sliced thinly and
    fronds reserved
175 g/6 oz mushrooms, sliced thinly
175 g/6 oz peeled, cooked prawns
pinch of cayenne pepper
300 ml/10 fl oz Béchamel Sauce
    (see page 14)
55 g/2 oz freshly grated Parmesan cheese
2 large tomatoes, sliced
1 tsp dried oregano
salt and pepper

1 Bring a saucepan of salted water to the boil. Add the pasta and oil and cook until tender, but still firm to the bite, according to packet instructions. Drain and return to the pan. Add 25 g/1 oz of butter, cover, shake the pan and keep the pasta warm.

2 Melt the remaining butter in a saucepan. Fry the fennel for 3–4 minutes. Stir in the mushrooms and fry for a further 2 minutes. Stir in the prawns, then remove from the heat.

3 Stir the cayenne pepper and prawn mixture into the Béchamel sauce, add the pasta and mix well to coat the pasta in the sauce. Pour into a greased ovenproof dish and spread out evenly. Sprinkle over the Parmesan cheese and arrange the tomato slices in a ring around the edge. Brush the tomatoes with olive oil and sprinkle over the oregano.

4 Bake in a preheated oven at 180°C/350°F/Gas Mark 4 for 25 minutes, or until golden brown. Serve immediately.

NUTRITION

Calories *478*; Sugars *6 g*; Protein *27 g*;
Carbohydrate *57 g*; Fat *17 g*; Saturates *7 g*

moderate

20 mins

45 mins

🍴 COOK'S TIP

This dish can be made in advance, then kept in the refrigerator until needed. It can also be frozen without the tomatoes, and cooked when required.

Popular in fishing ports around Europe, gentle stewing is an excellent way to maintain the flavour and succulent texture of fish and shellfish.

Mediterranean Fish Stew

1 Heat the oil in a large non-stick saucepan and fry the onions and garlic gently for 3 minutes.

2 Stir in the vinegar and sugar and cook for a further 2 minutes.

3 Stir in the stock, wine, tomatoes, aubergines courgettes, pepper and rosemary. Bring to the boil and simmer, uncovered, for 10 minutes.

4 Slice the squid into rings. Add the halibut, mussels and squid. Mix well and simmer, covered, for 5 minutes until the fish is opaque.

5 Stir in the prawns and continue to simmer, covered, for a further 2–3 minutes until the prawns are pink and cooked through.

6 Discard any mussels which haven't opened and season to taste.

7 To serve, put a slice of the toasted French bread rubbed with a cut garlic clove in the base of each warmed serving bowl and ladle the stew over the top. Serve with lemon wedges.

SERVES 4

2 tbsp olive oil
2 red onions, sliced
2 garlic cloves, crushed
2 tbsp red wine vinegar
2 tsp caster sugar
300 ml/10 fl oz Fresh Fish Stock
  (see page 16)
300 ml/10 fl oz dry red wine
800 g/1 lb 12 oz canned chopped tomatoes
225 g/8 oz baby aubergines, quartered
225 g/8 oz yellow courgettes, sliced
1 green pepper, sliced
1 tbsp chopped fresh rosemary
225 g/8 oz baby squid, cleaned and trimmed
500 g/1 lb 2 oz halibut fillet, skinned and cut
  into 2.5-cm/1-inch cubes
750 g/1 lb 10 oz fresh mussels, prepared
225 g/8 oz fresh raw tiger prawns, prepared
salt and pepper
4 slices toasted French bread rubbed with
  a cut garlic clove
lemon wedges, to serve

NUTRITION

Calories 533; Sugars 11 g; Protein 71 g;
Carbohydrate 30 g; Fat 10 g; Saturates 2 g

⭐⭐⭐⭒ challenging

🕐 1 hr

🕐 25 mins

PASTA & ITALIAN

This flavoursome and colourful fish pie is perfect for a light supper. The addition of smoked salmon gives it a touch of luxury.

Smoky Fish Pie

SERVES 4

900 g/2 lb smoked haddock or cod fillets
600 ml/1 pint skimmed milk
2 bay leaves
115 g/4 oz button mushrooms, quartered
115 g/4 oz frozen peas
115 g/4 oz frozen sweetcorn kernels
675 g/1½ lb potatoes, diced
5 tbsp low-fat natural yogurt
4 tbsp chopped fresh parsley
55 g/2 oz smoked salmon, sliced into thin strips
3 tbsp cornflour
25 g/1 oz smoked cheese, grated
salt and pepper

1 Preheat the oven to 200°C/400°F/Gas Mark 6. Place the fish in a large saucepan and add the milk and bay leaves. Bring to the boil, cover and then simmer for 5 minutes.

2 Add the mushrooms, peas and sweetcorn, bring back to a simmer, cover and cook for 5–7 minutes. Leave to cool.

3 Place the potatoes in a saucepan, cover with water, boil and cook for 8 minutes. Drain well and mash with a fork or a potato masher. Stir in the yogurt, parsley and seasoning. Set aside.

4 Using a slotted spoon, remove the fish from the pan. Flake the cooked fish away from the skin and place in an ovenproof gratin dish. Reserve the cooking liquid.

5 Drain the vegetables, reserving the cooking liquid, and gently stir into the fish with the salmon strips.

6 Blend a little cooking liquid into the cornflour to make a paste. Transfer the rest of the liquid to a saucepan and add the paste. Heat through, stirring, until thickened. Discard the bay leaves and season to taste. Pour the sauce over the fish and vegetables and mix. Spoon over the mashed potato so that the fish is covered, sprinkle with cheese and bake for 25–30 minutes.

NUTRITION

Calories 523; Sugars 15 g; Protein 58 g; Carbohydrate 63 g; Fat 6 g; Saturates 2 g

 challenging

 15 mins

1 hr

Use smoked cod or haddock in this delicious lasagne. It's a great way to make a little go a long way.

Smoked Fish Lasagne

1 Heat the oil in a saucepan and fry the garlic and onion for about 5 minutes. Add the mushrooms and cook for 3 minutes, stirring.

2 Add the tomatoes, courgette and stock or water and simmer, uncovered, for 15–20 minutes until the vegetables are soft. Season.

3 Put the butter or margarine, milk and flour into a small saucepan and heat, whisking constantly, until the sauce boils and thickens. Remove from the heat and add half of the cheese and all of the parsley. Stir gently to melt the cheese and season to taste.

4 Spoon the tomato sauce mixture into a large, shallow ovenproof dish and top with half of the lasagne sheets. Scatter the chunks of fish evenly over the top, then pour over half of the cheese sauce. Top with the remaining lasagne sheets and then spread the rest of the cheese sauce on top. Sprinkle with the remaining cheese.

5 Bake in a preheated oven, at 190°C/375°F/Gas Mark 5, for 40 minutes, until the top is golden brown and bubbling. Garnish with parsley sprigs and serve hot.

SERVES 4

2 tbsp olive or vegetable oil
1 garlic clove, crushed
1 small onion, chopped finely
125 g/4½ oz mushrooms, sliced
400 g/14 oz canned chopped tomatoes
1 small courgette, sliced
150 ml/¼ pint vegetable stock or water
25 g/1 oz butter or margarine
300 ml/10 fl oz skimmed milk
25 g/1 oz plain flour
125 g/4 oz grated mature Cheddar cheese
1 tbsp chopped fresh parsley
125 g/4½ oz (6 sheets) precooked lasagne
350 g/12 oz skinned and boned smoked cod or haddock, cut into chunks
salt and pepper
fresh parsley sprigs, to garnish

🕮 COOK'S TIP

You can use almost any variety of fish in this recipe but smoked fish adds a very special flavour.

NUTRITION
Calories 483; Sugars 8 g; Protein 36 g; Carbohydrate 32 g; Fat 24 g; Saturates 12 g

✪✪✪   moderate
🕐   20 mins
🕐   1 hr 15 mins

This is the ideal dish for a planned dinner party because the parcels can be prepared in advance, then put in the oven when you are ready to eat.

Pasta *and* Prawn Parcels

SERVES 4

450 g/1 lb dried fettuccine
2 quantities of Pesto Sauce (see page 133)
4 tsp extra virgin olive oil
750 g/1 lb 10 oz large raw prawns, peeled and deveined
2 garlic cloves, crushed
125 ml/4 fl oz dry white wine
salt and pepper

1 Cut out 4 30-cm/12-inch squares of greaseproof paper.

2 Bring a large saucepan of lightly salted water to the boil. Add the fettuccine and cook for 2–3 minutes, until just softened. Drain and set aside.

3 Mix together the fettuccine and half of the Pesto Sauce. Spread out the paper squares and put 1 teaspoon of olive oil in the middle of each. Divide the fettuccine between the squares, then divide the prawns and place on top of the fettuccine.

4 Mix together the remaining Pesto Sauce and the garlic and spoon it over the prawns. Season each parcel with salt and pepper and sprinkle with the white wine.

5 Dampen the edges of the greaseproof paper and wrap the parcels loosely, twisting the edges to seal.

6 Place the parcels on a baking tray and bake in a preheated oven at 200°C/400°F/Gas Mark 6 for 10–15 minutes. Transfer the parcels to 4 individual serving plates and serve.

NUTRITION

Calories *640*; Sugars *1 g*; Protein *50 g*; Carbohydrate *42 g*; Fat *29 g*; Saturates *4 g*

 moderate

 20 mins

20 mins

COOK'S TIP

Traditionally, these parcels are designed to look like money bags. The resemblance is more effective with greaseproof paper than with foil.

A luxurious dish which makes an impressive starter or light meal. Prawns and garlic are a winning combination.

Pan-Fried Prawns

1 Wash the prawns and pat dry using kitchen paper.

2 Melt the butter with the oil in a large frying pan, add the garlic and prawns, and fry over a high heat, stirring, for 3–4 minutes until the prawns are pink.

3 Sprinkle with brandy and season with salt and pepper to taste. Sprinkle with parsley and serve immediately with lemon wedges and ciabatta bread.

S E R V E S   4

4 garlic cloves, peeled and sliced
20–24 unshelled large raw prawns
125 g/4½ oz butter
4 tbsp olive oil
6 tbsp brandy
salt and pepper
2 tbsp chopped fresh parsley

to serve
lemon wedges
ciabatta bread

N U T R I T I O N
Calories 455; Sugars 0 g; Protein 6 g;
Carbohydrate 0 g; Fat 37 g; Saturates 18 g

  very easy

  10 mins

5 mins

Whole squid are stuffed with a mixture of fresh herbs and sun-dried tomatoes and then cooked in a wine sauce.

Squid *with* Wine *and* Rosemary

SERVES 4

8 squid, cleaned and gutted, but left whole
6 canned anchovies, chopped
2 garlic cloves, chopped
2 tbsp chopped rosemary leaves
2 sun-dried tomatoes, chopped
150 g/5½ oz breadcrumbs
1 tbsp olive oil
1 onion, finely chopped
200 ml/7 fl oz white wine
200 ml/7 fl oz Fresh Fish Stock (see page 16)
cooked rice, to serve
fresh rosemary sprigs, to garnish

1 Remove the tentacles from the squid bodies and chop them finely.

2 Grind the anchovies, garlic, rosemary and tomatoes to a paste in a mortar and pestle.

3 Add the breadcrumbs and the chopped squid tentacles and mix. If the mixture is too dry to form a thick paste at this point, add about 1 teaspoon of water.

4 Spoon the paste into the body sacs of the squid, then tie a length of cotton around the end of each sac to fasten. Do not overfill the sacs, because the filling will expand during cooking.

5 Heat the oil in a frying pan. Add the onion and cook, stirring, for 3–4 minutes, or until golden.

6 Add the stuffed squid to the pan and cook for 3–4 minutes, or until they are brown all over.

7 Add the wine and stock and bring to the boil. Reduce the heat, cover and then leave to simmer for 15 minutes.

8 Remove the lid and cook for a further 5 minutes, or until the squid is tender and the juices reduced. Garnish with rosemary sprigs, and serve with rice.

NUTRITION
Calories 276; Sugars 1 g; Protein 23 g;
Carbohydrate 20 g; Fat 8 g; Saturates 1 g

moderate

25 mins

35 mins

This is one of those dishes that looks almost too lovely to eat – but you simply have to eat it!

Farfallini Buttered Lobster

1 Carefully discard the stomach sac, vein and gills from each lobster. Remove all the meat from the tail and chop. Crack the claws and legs, remove the meat and chop. Transfer the meat to a bowl and add the lemon juice and grated lemon rind.

2 Clean the shells thoroughly and place in a warm oven at 160°C/325°/Gas Mark 3 to dry out.

3 Melt 25 g/1 oz of the butter in a frying pan. Add the breadcrumbs and fry for about 3 minutes, or until crisp and golden brown.

4 Melt the remaining butter in a saucepan. Add the lobster meat and heat through gently. Add the brandy and cook for a further 3 minutes, then add the cream and season to taste with salt and pepper.

5 Meanwhile, bring a large saucepan of lightly salted water to the boil. Add the farfallini and olive oil and cook for about 12 minutes, or until tender, but still firm to the bite. Drain and spoon the pasta into the clean lobster shells. Top with the buttered lobster and sprinkle with a little grated Parmesan cheese and the breadcrumbs. Grill for 2–3 minutes, or until golden brown.

6 Transfer the lobster shells to a warm serving dish, garnish with the lemon slices, kiwi fruit, king prawns and dill sprigs and serve immediately.

SERVES 4

2 x 700 g/1 lb 8 oz lobsters, split into halves
juice and grated rind of 1 lemon
115 g/4 oz butter
4 tbsp fresh white breadcrumbs
2 tbsp brandy
5 tbsp double cream or crème fraîche
450 g/1 lb dried farfallini
1 tbsp olive oil
55 g/2 oz freshly grated Parmesan cheese
salt and pepper

to garnish
1 kiwi fruit, sliced
4 unpeeled, cooked king prawns
fresh dill sprigs

NUTRITION
Calories *686*; Sugars *1 g*; Protein *45 g*;
Carbohydrate *44 g*; Fat *36 g*; Saturates *19 g*

 moderate

30 mins

25 mins

A quickly cooked recipe
that transforms
store-cupboard ingredients
into a dish with style.

Vermicelli *with* Clams

SERVES 4

400 g/14 oz dried vermicelli, spaghetti or
   other long pasta
2 tbsp olive oil
25 g/1 oz butter
2 onions, chopped
2 garlic cloves, chopped
2 x 200 g/7 oz jars clams in brine
125 ml/4 fl oz white wine
4 tbsp chopped fresh parsley
½ tsp dried oregano
pinch of freshly grated nutmeg
salt and pepper

to garnish
2 tbsp Parmesan cheese shavings
fresh basil sprigs

1 Bring a large saucepan of lightly salted water to the boil. Add the pasta and half the olive oil and cook until tender, but still firm to the bite. Drain, return to the pan and add the butter. Cover the saucepan, shake it well and keep warm.

2 Heat the remaining oil in a pan over a medium heat. Add the onions and fry until they are translucent. Stir in the garlic and cook for 1 minute.

3 Strain the liquid from 1 jar of clams and add it to the pan, with the wine. Stir, bring to simmering point and simmer for 3 minutes. Drain the second jar of clams and discard the liquid.

4 Add the clams, parsley and oregano to the pan and season with pepper and nutmeg. Lower the heat and cook until the sauce is heated through.

5 Transfer the pasta to a warm serving dish and pour over the sauce. Sprinkle with the Parmesan cheese, garnish with the basil and serve at once.

NUTRITION
Calories 520; Sugars 2 g; Protein 26 g;
Carbohydrate 71 g; Fat 13 g; Saturates 4 g

easy

10 mins

25 mins

🍷 **COOK'S TIP**

There are many different types of clams found along almost every coast in the world. Those traditionally used in this dish are the tiny ones – only 2.5–5 cm/ 1–2 inches across — known in Italy as vongole.

This is another tempting seafood dish where the eye is delighted as much as the tastebuds.

Baked Scallops *with* Pasta in Shells

1 Remove the scallops from their shells. Scrape off the skirt and the black intestinal thread. Reserve the white part (the flesh) and the orange part (the coral or roe). Very carefully ease the flesh and coral from the shell with a short, but very strong knife.

2 Wash the shells thoroughly and dry them well. Put the shells on a baking tray, sprinkle lightly with about two thirds of the olive oil and set aside.

3 Meanwhile, bring a large saucepan of lightly salted water to the boil. Add the pasta shells and remaining olive oil and cook for about 12 minutes, or until tender, but still firm to the bite. Drain and spoon about 25 g/1 oz of pasta into each scallop shell.

4 Put the scallops, fish stock and onion in an ovenproof dish and season to taste with pepper. Cover with foil and bake in a preheated oven at 180°C/350°F/Gas Mark 4 for 8 minutes.

5 Remove the dish from the oven. Remove the foil then use a slotted spoon to transfer the scallops to the shells. Add 1 tbsp of the cooking liquid to each shell, together with a drizzle of lemon juice, a little lemon rind and cream, and top with the Cheddar cheese.

6 Increase the oven temperature to 230°C/450°F/Gas Mark 8 and return the scallops to the oven for a further 4 minutes.

7 Serve the scallops in their shells with crusty brown bread and butter.

SERVES 4

12 scallops
3 tbsp olive oil
350 g/12 oz small, dried wholemeal pasta shells
150 ml/5 fl oz Fresh Fish Stock (see page 16)
1 onion, chopped
juice and finely grated rind of 2 lemons
150 ml/5 fl oz double cream
225 g/8 oz grated Cheddar cheese
salt and pepper
crusty brown bread, to serve

NUTRITION
Calories 725; Sugars 2 g; Protein 38 g; Carbohydrate 38 g; Fat 48 g; Saturates 25 g

  moderate

20 mins

30 mins

Meat

Italians have their very own special way of butchering meat, producing very different cuts. Most meat is sold ready-boned and often cut straight across the grain. Veal is a great favourite and widely available. Pork is also popular, with roast pig being the traditional dish of Umbria. Suckling pig is roasted with lots of fresh herbs, especially rosemary, until the skin is crisp and brown. Lamb is often served for special occasions, cooked on a spit or roasted in the oven with wine, garlic and herbs; and the very small cutlets from young lambs feature widely, especially in Rome. Offal plays an important role, too, with liver, brains, sweetbreads, tongue, heart, tripe and kidneys always available. Whatever your favourite Italian meat dish is, it's sure to be included in this chapter.

Barolo is a famous wine from the Piedmont area of Italy. Its mellow flavour is the key to this dish, so don't stint on the quality of the wine.

Beef *in* Barolo

SERVES 4

4 tbsp oil
1 kg/2 lb 4 oz piece boned rolled rib of beef, or piece of silverside
2 garlic cloves, crushed
4 shallots, sliced
1 tsp chopped fresh rosemary
1 tsp chopped fresh oregano
2 celery sticks, sliced
1 large carrot, diced
2 whole cloves
1 bottle Barolo wine
freshly grated nutmeg
salt and pepper
cooked vegetables, such as broccoli, carrots and new potatoes, to serve

1 Heat the oil in a flameproof casserole and brown the meat all over. Remove the meat from the casserole.

2 Add the garlic, shallots, herbs, celery, carrot and cloves and fry for 5 minutes.

3 Replace the meat on top of the vegetables. Pour in the wine. Cover the casserole and simmer gently for about 2 hours until tender. Remove the meat from the casserole, leave to rest before slicing and keep warm.

4 Rub the contents of the pan through a sieve or purée in a food processor or blender, adding a little hot beef stock if necessary. Season with nutmeg, salt and pepper.

5 Serve the meat with the sauce and accompanied by cooked vegetables, such as broccoli, carrots and new potatoes.

NUTRITION
Calories *744*; Sugars *1 g*; Protein *66 g*;
Carbohydrate *1 g*; Fat *43 g*; Saturates *16 g*

 moderate

15 mins

2 hrs 15 mins

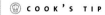 **COOK'S TIP**

If Barolo is unavailable, choose another full-bodied red wine instead.

Wafer-thin slices of tender beef with a rich garlic and bacon stuffing are flavoured with the tang of orange in this dish.

Beef Olives *in* Rich Gravy

1 Flatten out the beef olives as thinly as possible using a meat tenderizer or mallet. Trim the edges to neaten them.

2 Mix together the parsley, garlic, bacon, orange rind and salt and pepper to taste. Spread this mixture evenly over each beef olive.

3 Roll up each beef olive tightly, then secure with a cocktail stick. Heat the oil in a frying pan and fry the beef on all sides for 10 minutes.

4 Drain the beef olives, reserving the pan juices, and keep warm. Pour the wine into the juices, add the bay leaf, sugar and seasoning. Bring to the boil and boil rapidly for 5 minutes to reduce slightly, stirring.

5 Return the cooked beef to the pan along with the black olives and heat through for a further 2 minutes. Discard the bay leaf and cocktail sticks.

6 Transfer the beef olives and gravy to a serving dish, and serve garnished with orange slices and parsley.

S E R V E S **4**

8 ready prepared beef olives (available from your butcher)
4 tbsp chopped fresh parsley
4 garlic cloves, chopped finely
125 g/4$\frac{1}{2}$ oz smoked streaky bacon, de-rinded and chopped finely
grated rind of $\frac{1}{2}$ small orange
2 tbsp olive oil
300 ml/10 fl oz dry red wine
1 bay leaf
1 tsp sugar
55 g/2 oz stoned black olives, drained
salt and pepper

to garnish
orange slices
chopped fresh parsley

N U T R I T I O N
Calories *379*; Sugars *4 g*; Protein *26 g*;
Carbohydrate *4 g*; Fat *24 g*; Saturates *8 g*

moderate

20 mins

20 mins

In this recipe the 'pasta' dough is made with potatoes instead of flour. The small round ravioli are filled with a rich Bolognese sauce.

Beef *and* Potato Ravioli

SERVES 4

filling
1 tbsp vegetable oil
125 g/4½ oz minced beef
1 shallot, diced
1 garlic clove, crushed
1 tbsp plain flour
1 tbsp tomato purée
150 ml/5 fl oz beef stock
1 celery stick, chopped
2 tomatoes, peeled and diced
2 tsp chopped fresh basil
salt and pepper

ravioli
450 g/1 lb floury potatoes, diced
3 small egg yolks
3 tbsp olive oil
175 g/6 oz plain flour
55 g/2 oz butter, for frying
shredded fresh basil leaves, to garnish

NUTRITION
Calories *618*; Sugars *4 g*; Protein *16 g*;
Carbohydrate *74 g*; Fat *31 g*; Saturates *12 g*

✪✪✪✪ challenging
🕐 30 mins
🕐 50 mins

1 To make the filling, heat the vegetable oil in a large frying pan and fry the beef for 3–4 minutes, breaking it up with a spoon.

2 Add the shallots and garlic to the pan and cook for 2–3 minutes, or until the shallots have softened.

3 Stir in the flour and tomato purée and cook for 1 minute. Stir in the beef stock, celery, tomatoes and basil. Season to taste with salt and pepper.

4 Cook the mixture over a low heat for 20 minutes. Remove from the heat and leave to cool.

5 To make the ravioli, cook the potatoes in a saucepan of boiling water for 10 minutes until cooked.

6 Mash the potatoes and place them in a mixing bowl. Blend in the egg yolks and oil. Season, then stir in the flour and mix to form a dough.

7 On a lightly floured surface, divide the dough into 24 pieces and shape into flat rounds. Spoon the filling on to one half of each round and fold the dough over to encase the filling, pressing down to seal the edges.

8 Melt the butter in a frying pan and cook the ravioli for 6–8 minutes, turning once, until golden. Serve hot, garnished with shredded basil leaves.

A different twist is given to this traditional pasta dish with a rich, but subtle sauce.

Meatballs *in* Red Wine Sauce

1 Pour the milk into a bowl and soak the breadcrumbs in the milk for 30 minutes.

2 Heat half of the butter and 4 tablespoons of the oil in a frying pan. Fry the mushrooms for 4 minutes, then stir in the flour and cook for 2 minutes. Add the stock and wine and simmer for 15 minutes. Add the tomatoes, tomato purée, sugar and basil. Season and simmer for 30 minutes.

3 Mix the shallots, steak and paprika with the breadcrumbs and season to taste. Shape the mixture into 14 meatballs.

4 Heat 4 tablespoons of the remaining oil and the remaining butter in a large frying pan. Fry the meatballs in batches, turning frequently, until brown all over. Transfer to a deep casserole, pour over the red wine and the mushroom sauce, cover and bake in a preheated oven, at 180°C/350°F/Gas Mark 4, for 30 minutes.

5 Bring a saucepan of salted water to the boil. Add the pasta and the remaining oil and cook for 8–10 minutes or until tender. Drain and transfer to a serving dish. Remove the casserole from the oven and cool for 3 minutes. Pour the meatballs and sauce on to the pasta, garnish and serve.

 COOK'S TIP

Choose a good quality, full-bodied red wine for this recipe, for extra flavour.

SERVES 4

150 ml/¼ pint milk
150 g/5½ oz white breadcrumbs
25 g/1 oz butter
125 ml/4 fl oz olive oil
225 g/8 oz oyster mushrooms, sliced
25 g/1 oz wholemeal flour
200 ml/7 fl oz beef stock
150 ml/¼ pint red wine
4 tomatoes, skinned and chopped
1 tbsp tomato purée
1 tsp brown sugar
1 tbsp finely chopped fresh basil
12 shallots, chopped
450 g/1 lb minced steak
1 tsp paprika
450 g/1 lb dried egg tagliarini
salt and pepper
fresh basil sprigs, to garnish

NUTRITION

Calories 811; Sugars 7 g; Protein 30 g; Carbohydrate 76 g; Fat 43 g; Saturates 12 g

●●● moderate
● 45 mins
● 1 hr 40 mins

The fresh taste of sage
is the perfect ingredient
to counteract the richness
of pork.

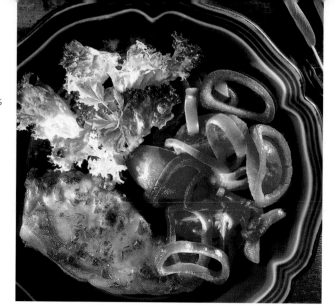

Pork Chops *with* Sage

SERVES 4

2 tbsp flour
1 tbsp chopped fresh sage or 1 tsp dried
4 lean boneless pork chops, trimmed of excess fat
2 tbsp olive oil
15 g/½ oz butter
2 red onions, sliced into rings
1 tbsp lemon juice
2 tsp caster sugar
4 plum tomatoes, quartered
salt and pepper
green salad, to serve

1 Mix the flour, sage and salt and pepper on a plate. Lightly dust the pork chops on both sides with the seasoned flour.

2 Heat the oil and butter in a frying pan, add the chops and cook them for 6–7 minutes on each side until cooked through. Drain the chops, reserving the pan juices, and keep warm.

3 Toss the onion in the lemon juice and fry along with the sugar and tomatoes for 5 minutes until tender.

4 Serve the pork with the tomato and onion mixture and a green salad.

NUTRITION
Calories *364*; Sugars *5 g*; Protein *34 g*;
Carbohydrate *14 g*; Fat *19 g*; Saturates *7 g*

 easy

 10 mins

10 mins

15 mins

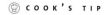 **COOK'S TIP**

If plum tomatoes are unavailable, choose ripe, but firm, large tomatoes instead.

This traditional dish of boned pork cooked with garlic and milk can be served hot or cold.

Pork Cooked *in* Milk

1 Using a sharp knife, remove the fat from the pork. Shape the meat into a neat form, tying it in place with a length of string.

2 Heat the oil and butter in a large saucepan. Add the onion, garlic and pancetta to the saucepan and cook for 2–3 minutes.

3 Add the pork to the saucepan and cook, turning occasionally, until it is browned all over.

4 Pour over the milk, add the peppercorns, bay leaves, marjoram and thyme and cook over a low heat for 1¼–1½ hours or until tender. Watch the liquid carefully for the last 15 minutes of cooking time because it tends to reduce very quickly and will burn. If the liquid reduces and the pork is still not tender, add another 100 ml/3½ fl oz milk and continue cooking. Reserve the cooking liquid (as the milk reduces naturally in this dish, it forms a thick and creamy sauce, which curdles slightly but tastes delicious).

5 Remove the pork from the saucepan. Using a sharp knife, cut the meat into slices. Transfer the pork slices to serving plates and serve immediately with the reserved cooking liquid as a sauce.

S E R V E S   4

800 g/1 lb 12 oz leg of pork, boned
1 tbsp oil
25 g/1 oz butter
1 onion, chopped
2 garlic cloves, chopped
75 g/2¾ oz pancetta, diced
1.2 litres/2 pints milk
1 tbsp green peppercorns, crushed
2 fresh bay leaves
2 tbsp fresh chopped marjoram
2 tbsp fresh chopped thyme

N U T R I T I O N
Calories *498*; Sugars *15 g*; Protein *50 g*;
Carbohydrate *15 g*; Fat *27 g*; Saturates *9 g*

 moderate
 20 mins
1 hr 45 mins

This is a simplified version
of a traditional dish from
the Marche region of Italy.
Pork fillet pockets are
stuffed with ham
(prosciutto) and herbs.

Pork *with* Lemon *and* Garlic

S E R V E S 4

450 g/1 lb pork fillet
50 g/1³/₄ oz chopped almonds
2 tbsp olive oil
100 g/3¹/₂ oz raw Parma ham, finely chopped
2 garlic cloves, chopped
1 tbsp fresh oregano, chopped
finely grated rind of 2 lemons
4 shallots, finely chopped
200 ml/7 fl oz ham or chicken stock
1 tsp sugar

1 Using a sharp knife, cut the pork fillet into 4 equal pieces. Place the pork between sheets of greaseproof paper and pound each piece with a meat mallet or the end of a rolling pin to flatten it.

2 Cut a horizontal slit in each piece of pork to make a pocket.

3 Place the almonds on a baking tray. Lightly toast the almonds under a medium–hot grill for 2–3 minutes or until golden.

4 Mix the almonds with 1 tablespoon of olive oil, ham, garlic, oregano and the grated rind from 1 lemon. Spoon the mixture into the pockets of the pork.

5 Heat the remaining olive oil in a large frying pan. Add the shallots and cook for 2 minutes.

6 Add the pork to the frying pan and cook for 2 minutes on each side or until browned all over.

7 Add the stock to the pan, bring to the boil, cover and leave to simmer for 45 minutes or until the pork is tender. Remove the meat from the pan, set aside and keep warm.

8 Add the remaining lemon rind and sugar to the pan and boil for 3–4 minutes or until reduced and syrupy. Pour the lemon sauce over the pork fillets and serve immediately.

N U T R I T I O N
Calories *428*; Sugars *2 g*; Protein *31 g*;
Carbohydrate *4 g*; Fat *32 g*; Saturates *4 g*

moderate

25 mins

1 hr

This sophisticated roast with Mediterranean flavours is delicious served with a pungent olive paste.

Pork Stuffed *with* Prosciutto

1 Trim away any excess fat and membrane from the pork fillet. Slice the pork lengthways down the middle, taking care not to cut all the way through.

2 Open out the pork and season the inside with salt and pepper. Lay the basil leaves down the centre. Mix the cheese and sun-dried tomato paste and spread over the basil.

3 Press the pork back together. Wrap the ham around the pork, overlapping, to cover. Place on a rack in a roasting tin, seamside down, and brush with oil. Bake in a preheated oven,190°C/375°F/Gas Mark 5, for 30–40 minutes, depending on thickness, until cooked through. Allow to stand for 10 minutes.

4 For the olive paste, place all the ingredients in a blender or food processor and process until smooth. Alternatively, for a coarser paste, finely chop the olives and garlic and mix with the oil.

5 Drain the cooked pork and slice. Serve with the olive paste and a salad.

SERVES 4

500 g/1 lb 2 oz piece of lean pork fillet
small bunch of fresh basil leaves, washed
2 tbsp freshly grated Parmesan cheese
2 tbsp sun-dried tomato paste
6 thin slices Parma ham
1 tbsp olive oil
salt and pepper
salad leaves, to serve

olive paste

125 g/4 oz stoned black olives
4 tbsp olive oil
2 garlic cloves, peeled

NUTRITION
Calories *427*; Sugars *0 g*; Protein *31 g*;
Carbohydrate *0.2 g*; Fat *34 g*; Saturates *7 g*

moderate

25 mins

30-40 mins

👑 **COOK'S TIP**

Choose a good lean piece of pork fillet for the best results.

PASTA & ITALIAN

Cannelloni, the thick,
round pasta tubes,
make perfect containers
for close-textured sauces
of all kinds.

Spinach, Cheese *and* Ham Cannelloni

SERVES 4

8 dried cannelloni tubes
1 tbsp olive oil
25 g/1 oz freshly grated Parmesan cheese
fresh herb sprigs, to garnish

filling
25 g/1 oz butter
300 g/10½ oz frozen spinach, thawed
    and chopped
115 g/4 oz ricotta cheese
25 g/1 oz freshly grated Parmesan cheese
55 g/2 oz chopped ham
pinch of freshly grated nutmeg
2 tbsp double cream
2 eggs, lightly beaten
salt and pepper

sauce
25 g/1 oz butter
25 g/1 oz plain flour
300 ml/10 fl oz milk
2 bay leaves
pinch of freshly grated nutmeg

NUTRITION
Calories 520; Sugars 5 g; Protein 21 g;
Carbohydrate 23 g; Fat 39 g; Saturates 18 g

moderate

30 mins

1 hr 15 mins

1 To make the filling, melt the butter in a pan and stir-fry the spinach for
2–3 minutes. Remove from the heat and stir in the ricotta and Parmesan
cheeses, and the ham. Season to taste with nutmeg, salt and pepper. Beat in
the cream and eggs to make a thick paste.

2 Bring a saucepan of lightly salted water to the boil. Add the cannelloni
tubes and the oil and cook for 10–12 minutes, or until almost tender. Drain
and set aside to cool.

3 To make the sauce, melt the butter in a pan. Stir in the flour and cook,
stirring, for 1 minute. Gradually stir in the milk. Add the bay leaves and
simmer, stirring, for 5 minutes. Add the nutmeg and salt and pepper to
taste. Remove from the heat and discard the bay leaves.

4 Spoon the filling into a piping bag and fill the cannelloni.

5 Spoon a little sauce into the base of an ovenproof dish. Arrange the
cannelloni in the dish in a single layer and pour over the remaining sauce.
Sprinkle over the Parmesan cheese and bake in a preheated oven at
190°C/375°F/Gas Mark 5 for 40–45 minutes. Garnish with fresh herb sprigs
and serve.

An Italian version of grilled pork steaks, this dish is delicious and easy to make.

Neopolitan Pork Steaks

1 Heat the oil in a large frying pan. Add the onions and garlic and cook, stirring, for 3–4 minutes, or until they just begin to soften.

2 Add the tomatoes and yeast extract to the frying pan and leave to simmer for about 5 minutes, or until the sauce starts to thicken.

3 Cook the pork steaks, under a preheated grill for 5 minutes on both sides, or until the the meat is golden and cooked through. Set the pork steaks aside and keep warm.

4 Add the olives and fresh shredded basil to the sauce in the frying pan and stir quickly to combine.

5 Transfer the pork steaks to warm serving plates. Top the steaks with the sauce and sprinkle with freshly grated Parmesan cheese, then serve immediately with vegetables of your choice.

SERVES 4

2 tbsp olive oil
1 large onion, sliced
1 garlic clove, chopped
400 g/14 oz canned tomatoes
2 tsp yeast extract
4 pork loin steaks, about 125 g/4½ oz each
75 g/2¾ oz black olives, stoned
2 tbsp shredded fresh basil

to serve
freshly grated Parmesan cheese
fresh vegetables

NUTRITION
Calories *353*; Sugars *3 g*; Protein *39 g*;
Carbohydrate *4 g*; Fat *20 g*; Saturates *5 g*

easy

10 mins

25 mins

(👨) **COOK'S TIP**

Parmesan is a mature and exceptionally hard cheese produced in Italy. You only need to use a little as it has a very strong flavour.

PASTA & ITALIAN

Chunks of tender lamb, pan-fried with garlic and stewed in red wine are a real Roman dish.

Lamb *and* Anchovies *with* Thyme

SERVES 4

1 tbsp oil
15 g/½ oz butter
600 g/1 lb 5 oz lamb (shoulder or leg), cut into 2.5-cm/1-inch chunks
4 garlic cloves, peeled
3 fresh thyme sprigs, stalks removed
6 canned anchovy fillets
150 ml/5 fl oz red wine
150 ml/5 fl oz lamb or vegetable stock
1 tsp sugar
50 g/1¾ oz black olives, stoned and halved
2 tbsp chopped fresh parsley, to garnish

1 Heat the oil and butter in a large frying pan. Add the lamb and cook for 4–5 minutes, stirring, until the meat is browned all over.

2 Using a pestle and mortar, grind together the garlic, thyme and anchovies to make a smooth paste.

3 Add the wine and stock to the frying pan. Stir in the garlic and anchovy paste together with the sugar.

4 Bring the mixture to the boil, reduce the heat, cover and leave to simmer for 30–40 minutes, or until the lamb is tender. For the last 10 minutes of the cooking time, remove the lid in order to allow the sauce to reduce slightly.

5 Stir the olives into the sauce and mix to combine.

6 Transfer the lamb and its sauce to a serving bowl and garnish with chopped fresh parsley. Serve at once.

NUTRITION
Calories *299*; Sugars *1 g*; Protein *31 g*; Carbohydrate *1 g*; Fat *16 g*; Saturates *7 g*

 moderate
15 mins
50 mins

🍴 **COOK'S TIP**

This dish is excellent served with mashed or lightly sautéed potatoes.

M
E
A
T

This dish from the Abruzzi region uses a slow cooking method which ensures that the meat absorbs the flavourings and becomes very tender.

Pot Roasted Leg *of* Lamb

1 Wipe the leg of lamb all over, trimming off any excess fat, then season well with salt and pepper, rubbing it well in. Lay the sprigs of rosemary over the lamb, cover evenly with the bacon rashers and tie in place with string.

2 Heat the oil in a frying pan and fry the lamb for about 10 minutes or until browned all over, turning several times. Remove from the pan.

3 Transfer the oil from the frying pan to a large ovenproof casserole and fry the garlic and onion together for 3–4 minutes until beginning to soften. Add the carrots and celery and continue to cook for a few minutes longer.

4 Lay the lamb on top of the vegetables and press down to submerge partly. Pour the wine over the lamb, add the tomato purée and simmer for 3–4 minutes. Add the stock, tomatoes and herbs and seasoning and bring back to the boil for a further 3–4 minutes.

5 Cover the casserole tightly and cook in a moderate oven, 180°C/350°F/Gas Mark 4, for 2–2½ hours, until very tender.

6 Remove the lamb from the casserole and, if preferred, take off the bacon and herbs along with the string. Keep warm. Strain the juices, skimming off any excess fat, and serve in a jug. The vegetables may be put around the joint or in a separate dish. Garnish with fresh rosemary sprigs and serve.

SERVES 4

1.75 kg/3½ lb leg of lamb
3–4 fresh rosemary sprigs
125 g/4½ oz streaky bacon rashers
4 tbsp olive oil
2–3 garlic cloves, crushed
2 onions, sliced
2 carrots, sliced
2 celery sticks, sliced
300 ml/10 fl oz dry white wine
1 tbsp tomato purée
300 ml/10 fl oz stock
350 g/12 oz tomatoes, peeled, quartered and deseeded
1 tbsp chopped fresh parsley
1 tbsp chopped fresh oregano or marjoram
salt and pepper
fresh rosemary sprigs, to garnish

NUTRITION
Calories *734*; Sugars *6 g*; Protein *71 g*;
Carbohydrate *7 g*; Fat *42 g*; Saturates *15 g*

✪✪✪✪ challenging
 35 mins
 3 hrs

A classic combination of flavours, this dish would make a perfect Sunday lunch. Serve with tomato and onion salad and jacket potatoes.

Lamb Cutlets *with* Rosemary

SERVES 4

8 lamb cutlets
5 tbsp olive oil
2 tbsp lemon juice
1 garlic clove, crushed
½ tsp lemon pepper
8 fresh rosemary sprigs
salt
jacket potatoes, to serve

salad
4 tomatoes, sliced
4 spring onions, sliced diagonally

dressing
2 tbsp olive oil
1 tbsp lemon juice
1 garlic clove, chopped
¼ tsp finely chopped fresh rosemary

1 Trim the lamb chops by cutting away the flesh with a sharp knife to expose the tips of the bones.

2 Place the oil, lemon juice, garlic, lemon pepper and salt in a shallow, non-metallic dish and whisk with a fork to combine.

3 Lay the sprigs of rosemary in the dish and place the lamb on top. Leave to marinate for at least 1 hour, turning the lamb cutlets once.

4 Remove the chops from the marinade and wrap a little kitchen foil around the exposed bones to stop them from burning.

5 Place the sprigs of rosemary on the rack and place the lamb on top. Barbecue for 10–15 minutes, turning once.

6 Meanwhile, make the salad and dressing. Arrange the tomatoes on a serving dish and scatter the spring onions on top. Place all the ingredients for the dressing in a screw-top jar, shake well and pour over the salad. Serve with the barbecued lamb cutlets and jacket potatoes.

NUTRITION
Calories *560*; Sugars *1 g*; Protein *48 g*; Carbohydrate *1 g*; Fat *40 g*; Saturates *1 g*

moderate

1 hr 15 mins

15 mins

🍲 **COOK'S TIP**

Choose medium to small baking potatoes if you want to cook jacket potatoes on the barbecue. Scrub them well, prick with a fork and wrap in buttered kitchen foil. Bury them in the hot coals and barbecue for 50–60 minutes.

Lamb chops are more elegant when the bone is removed to make noisettes.

Lamb *with* Bay *and* Lemon

1 Using a sharp knife, carefully remove the bone from each lamb chop, keeping the meat intact. Alternatively, ask the butcher to prepare the lamb noisettes for you.

2 Shape the meat into rounds and secure with a length of string.

3 In a large frying pan, heat together the oil and butter until the mixture starts to froth.

4 Add the lamb noisettes to the frying pan and cook for 2–3 minutes on each side or until browned all over.

5 Remove the frying pan fom the heat, remove the meat, drain off all of the excess fat and discard. Place the noisettes back in the pan.

6 Return the frying pan to the heat. Add the wine, stock, bay leaves and lemon rind to the frying pan and cook for 20–25 minutes or until the lamb is tender. Season the lamb and sauce to taste with a little salt and pepper.

7 Transfer to serving plates. Remove the string from each noisette and serve with the sauce.

SERVES 4

4 lamb chops
1 tbsp oil
15 g/½ oz butter
150 ml/5 fl oz white wine
150 ml/5 fl oz lamb or vegetable stock
2 bay leaves
pared rind of 1 lemon
salt and pepper

NUTRITION
Calories *268*; Sugars *0.2 g*; Protein *24 g*;
Carbohydrate *0.2 g*; Fat *16 g*; Saturates *7 g*

 moderate

 10 mins

35 mins

The Italian name for this dish means 'jump into the mouth'. These stuffed rolls are quick and easy to make and taste delicious.

Saltimbocca

SERVES 4

4 turkey fillets or 4 veal escalopes, about 450 g/1 lb in total
100 g/3 ½ oz Parma ham
8 fresh sage leaves
1 tbsp olive oil
1 onion, chopped finely
200 ml/7 fl oz white wine
200 ml/7 fl oz chicken stock

1 Place the turkey or veal between sheets of greaseproof paper. Pound the meat with a meat mallet or the end of a rolling pin to flatten it slightly. Cut each escalope in half.

2 Trim the Parma ham to fit each piece of turkey or veal and place over the meat. Lay a sage leaf on top. Roll up the escalopes and secure the rolls with cocktail sticks.

3 Heat the oil in a frying pan and cook the onion for 3–4 minutes. Add the turkey or veal rolls to the pan and cook for 5 minutes, or until brown all over.

4 Pour the wine and stock into the pan and leave to simmer for 15 minutes if using turkey, and 20 minutes for veal, or until tender. Serve immediately.

NUTRITION
Calories 303; Sugars 0.3 g; Protein 29 g; Carbohydrate 1 g; Fat 17 g; Saturates 1 g

moderate
15 mins
25–30 mins

 COOK'S TIP

If using turkey rather than veal, watch it carefully as turkey tends to turn dry very quickly if overcooked.

The delicious combination of apple, onion and mushroom perfectly complements the delicate flavour of veal.

Neapolitan Veal Cutlets *and* Mascarpone

1 Melt 55 g/2 oz of the butter in a frying pan. Fry the veal over a low heat for 5 minutes on each side. Transfer to a dish and keep warm.

2 Fry the onion and apples in the pan until lightly browned. Transfer to a dish, place the veal on top and keep warm.

3 Melt the remaining butter in the frying pan. Gently fry the mushrooms, tarragon and peppercorns over a low heat for 3 minutes. Sprinkle over the sesame seeds.

4 Bring a saucepan of lightly salted water to the boil. Add the pasta and 1 tablespoon of the oil. Cook until tender, but still firm to the bite. Drain and transfer to a serving plate.

5 Top the pasta with teaspoonfuls of mascarpone and sprinkle over the remaining olive oil. Place the onions, apples and veal cutlets on top of the pasta. Spoon the mushrooms and peppercorns on to the cutlets and place the tomatoes and basil leaves around the edge. Place in a preheated oven at 150°C/300°F/Gas Mark 2, for 5 minutes.

6 Season to taste with salt and pepper, garnish with fresh basil leaves and serve immediately.

SERVES 4

200 g/7 oz butter
4 veal cutlets each about 250 g/9 oz, trimmed
1 large onion, sliced
2 apples, peeled, cored and sliced
175 g/6 oz button mushrooms
1 tbsp chopped fresh tarragon
8 black peppercorns
1 tbsp sesame seeds
400 g/14 oz dried marille pasta
100 ml/3½ fl oz extra-virgin olive oil
175 g/6 oz mascarpone cheese
salt and pepper
2 large beef tomatoes, cut in half
leaves of 1 fresh basil sprig
fresh basil leaves, to garnish

NUTRITION
Calories *1071*; Sugars *13 g*; Protein *74 g*; Carbohydrate *66 g*; Fat *59 g*; Saturates *16 g*

   moderate

20 mins

30 mins

This dish is really superb if made with tender veal. However, if veal is unavailable, use pork or turkey escalopes instead.

Veal Italienne

SERVES 4

55 g/2 oz butter
1 tbsp olive oil
675 g/1 lb 8 oz potatoes, cubed
4 veal escalopes, about 175 g/6 oz each
1 onion, cut into 8 wedges
2 garlic cloves, crushed
2 tbsp plain flour
2 tbsp tomato purée
150 ml/5 fl oz red wine
300 ml/10 fl oz chicken stock
8 ripe tomatoes, peeled, deseeded and diced
25 g/1 oz stoned black olives, halved
2 tbsp chopped fresh basil
salt and pepper
fresh basil leaves, to garnish

1 Heat the butter and oil in a large frying pan. Add the potatoes and cook for 5–7 minutes, stirring frequently, until they begin to brown.

2 Remove the potatoes from the pan with a slotted spoon and set aside.

3 Place the veal in the frying pan and cook for 2–3 minutes on each side, until sealed. Remove from the pan and set aside.

4 Stir the onion and garlic into the pan and cook for 2–3 minutes.

5 Add the flour and tomato purée and cook for 1 minute, stirring. Gradually blend in the red wine and chicken stock, stirring to make a smooth sauce.

6 Return the potatoes and veal to the pan. Stir in the tomatoes, olives and basil and season with salt and pepper.

7 Transfer to a casserole dish and cook in a preheated oven, 180°C/350°F/Gas Mark 4, for 1 hour or until the potatoes and veal are cooked through. Garnish with basil leaves and serve.

NUTRITION

Calories 592; Sugars 5 g; Protein 44 g;
Carbohydrate 48 g; Fat 23 g; Saturates 9 g

moderate

 25 mins

1 hr 20 mins

COOK'S TIP

For a quicker cooking time and really tender meat, pound the meat with a meat mallet or the end of a rolling pin to flatten it slightly before cooking.

Anchovies are often used to enhance flavour, particularly in meat dishes.

Escalopes *and* Italian Sausage

1 Heat the oil in a large frying pan. Add the anchovies, capers, fresh rosemary, orange rind and juice, Italian sausage and tomatoes to the pan and cook for 5–6 minutes, stirring occasionally.

2 Meanwhile, place the turkey or veal escalopes between sheets of greaseproof paper. Pound the meat with a meat mallet or the end of a rolling pin to flatten it.

3 Add the meat to the mixture in the frying pan. Season to taste with salt and pepper, cover and cook for 3–5 minutes on each side, slightly longer if the meat is thicker.

4 Transfer to serving plates and serve with fresh crusty bread.

SERVES 4

1 tbsp olive oil
6 canned anchovy fillets, drained
1 tbsp capers, drained
1 tbsp chopped fresh rosemary leaves
finely grated rind and juice of 1 orange
75 g/2³⁄4 oz Italian sausage, diced
3 tomatoes, skinned and chopped
4 turkey or veal escalopes, about
   125 g/4¹⁄2 oz each
salt and pepper
crusty bread or cooked polenta, to serve

NUTRITION

Calories *233*; Sugars *1 g*; Protein *28 g*;
Carbohydrate *1 g*; Fat *13 g*; Saturates *1 g*

 easy

 10 mins

 20 mins

👒 COOK'S TIP

Try using 4-minute steaks, slightly flattened, instead of the turkey or veal. Cook them for 4–5 minutes on top of the sauce in the pan.

In this traditional Tuscan dish, Italian sausages are cooked with cannellini beans and tomatoes.

Sausage *and* Bean Casserole

SERVES 4

8 Italian sausages
1 tbsp olive oil
1 large onion, chopped
2 garlic cloves, chopped
1 green pepper, halved, deseeded and cut into strips
225g/8 oz fresh tomatoes, skinned and chopped or 400 g/14 oz canned chopped tomatoes
2 tbsp sun-dried tomato paste
400 g/14 oz can cannellini beans
mashed potato or rice, to serve

1 Prick the Italian sausages all over with a fork. Cook the sausages, under a preheated grill, for 10–12 minutes, turning occasionally, until brown all over. Set aside and keep warm.

2 Heat the oil in a large frying pan. Add the onion, garlic and pepper to the frying pan and cook for 5 minutes, stirring occasionally, or until softened.

3 Add the tomatoes to the frying pan and leave the mixture to simmer for about 5 minutes, stirring occasionally, or until slightly reduced and thickened.

4 Stir the sun-dried tomato paste, cannellini beans and Italian sausages into the mixture in the frying pan. Cook for 4–5 minutes or until the mixture is piping hot. Add 4–5 tablespoons of water, if the mixture becomes too dry during cooking.

5 Transfer the Italian sausage and bean casserole to serving plates and serve with mashed potato or rice.

NUTRITION
Calories *600*; Sugars *7 g*; Protein *27 g*; Carbohydrate *20 g*; Fat *47 g*; Saturates *16 g*

easy

 15 mins

35 mins

 COOK'S TIP

Italian sausages are coarse in texture and have quite a strong flavour. They can be bought in specialist sausage shops, Italian delicatessens and some larger supermarkets. They are replaceable in this recipe only by game sausages.

Liver is popular in Italy and is served in many ways. Tender calf's liver is the best type to use for this recipe, but you could use lamb's liver.

Liver *with* Wine Sauce

1 Wipe the liver with kitchen paper, season with salt and pepper to taste and then coat lightly in flour, shaking off any excess.

2 Heat the oil and butter in a pan and fry the liver until well sealed on both sides and just cooked through (about 1 minute on each side) – take care not to overcook. Remove the liver from the pan, cover and keep warm, but do not allow to dry out.

3 Add the bacon to the fat left in the pan, with the garlic, onion and celery. Fry gently until the onion and celery are softened.

4 Add the red wine, beef stock, allspice, Worcestershire sauce, sage and salt and pepper to taste. Bring to the boil and simmer for 3–4 minutes.

5 Cut each tomato segment in half. Add to the sauce and continue to cook for 2–3 minutes.

6 Serve the liver on a little of the sauce, with the remainder spooned over. Garnish with fresh sage leaves and serve with new or sauté potatoes.

SERVES 4

4 slices calf's liver or 8 slices lamb's liver, about 500 g/1 lb 2 oz in total
flour, for coating
1 tbsp olive oil
25 g/1 oz butter
125 g/4½ oz lean bacon rashers, de-rinded and cut into narrow strips
1 garlic clove, crushed
1 onion, chopped
1 celery stick, sliced thinly
150 ml/5 fl oz red wine
150 ml/5 fl oz beef stock
good pinch of ground allspice
1 tsp Worcestershire sauce
1 tsp chopped fresh sage or ½ tsp dried sage
3–4 tomatoes, peeled, quartered and deseeded
salt and pepper
fresh sage leaves, to garnish
new potatoes or sauté potatoes, to serve

NUTRITION

Calories 435; Sugars 2 g; Protein 30 g; Carbohydrate 4 g; Fat 31 g; Saturates 12 g

 moderate

 25 mins

25 mins

20 mins

Chicken *and* Poultry

Poultry dishes provide some of Italy's finest food. Every part of the chicken is used, including the feet and innards for making soup. Spit-roasted chicken, strongly flavoured with aromatic rosemary, has become almost a national dish. Turkey, capon, duck, goose and guinea fowl are also popular, as is game. Wild rabbit, hare, wild boar and deer are available, especially in Sardinia. This chapter contains a superb collection of mouthwatering recipes. You will be astonished at how quickly and easily you can prepare some of these gourmet dishes.

A mixture of cheese, rosemary and sun-dried tomatoes is stuffed under the chicken skin, then roasted with garlic, potatoes and vegetables.

Mediterranean-Style Sunday Roast

SERVES 4

2.5 kg/5 lb 8 oz whole chicken
fresh rosemary sprigs
175 g/6 oz feta cheese, coarsely crumbled
2 tbsp sun-dried tomato purée
55 g/2 oz butter, softened
1 garlic bulb
1 kg/2 lb 4 oz new potatoes, halved if large
1 each red, green and yellow pepper, halved
    deseeded and cut into chunks
3 courgettes, sliced thinly
2 tbsp olive oil
2 tbsp plain flour
600 ml/1 pint chicken stock
salt and pepper

NUTRITION

Calories *488*; Sugars *6 g*; Protein *37 g*;
Carbohydrate *34 g*; Fat *23 g*; Saturates *11 g*

●●●   moderate

●   35 mins

●   1 hr 30 mins

1 Rinse the chicken inside and out with cold water and drain well. Carefully cut between the skin and the top of the breast meat using a small pointed knife. Slide a finger into the slit and carefully enlarge it to form a pocket. Continue until the skin is completely lifted away from both breasts and the top of the legs.

2 Chop the leaves from 3 rosemary sprigs. Mix with the feta cheese, sun-dried tomato purée, butter and pepper to taste, then spoon under the skin. Put the chicken in a large roasting tin, cover with foil and cook in a preheated oven, 190°C/375°F/Gas Mark 5, for 20 minutes per 500 g/1 lb 2 oz, plus 20 minutes.

3 Break the garlic bulb into cloves but do not peel. Add the garlic and vegetables to the chicken in the tin after 40 minutes.

4 Drizzle with oil, tuck in a few rosemary sprigs and season with salt and pepper. Cook for the remaining calculated time, removing the foil for the last 40 minutes to brown the chicken.

5 Transfer the chicken to a serving platter. Place some of the vegetables around the chicken and transfer the remainder to a warmed serving dish. Pour the fat out of the roasting tin and stir the flour into the remaining pan juices. Cook for 2 minutes then gradually stir in the stock. Bring to the boil, stirring until thickened. Strain into a sauce boat and serve with the chicken and vegetables.

There is a delicious surprise of creamy herb and garlic soft cheese hidden inside these chicken parcels!

Garlic *and* Herb Chicken

1 Using a sharp knife, make a horizontal slit along the length of each chicken breast to form a pocket.

2 Beat the cheese with a wooden spoon to soften it. Spoon the cheese into the pocket of the chicken breasts.

3 Wrap 2 slices of Parma ham around each chicken breast and secure firmly in place with a length of string.

4 Pour the wine and chicken stock into a large frying pan and bring to the boil. When just starting to boil, add the sugar and stir well to dissolve.

5 Add the chicken breasts to the mixture in the frying pan. Leave to simmer for 12–15 minutes or until the chicken is tender and the juices run clear when a skewer is inserted into the thickest part of the meat.

6 Remove the chicken from the pan, set aside and keep warm.

7 Reheat the sauce and boil until reduced and thickened. Remove the string from the chicken and cut into slices. Pour the sauce over the chicken and serve with a green salad.

S E R V E S   4

4 chicken breasts, skin removed
100 g/3½ oz full fat soft cheese, flavoured with herbs and garlic
8 slices Parma ham
150 ml/5 fl oz red wine
150 ml/5 fl oz chicken stock
1 tbsp brown sugar
green salad, to serve

N U T R I T I O N

Calories 272; Sugars 4 g; Protein 29 g; Carbohydrate 4 g; Fat 13 g; Saturates 6 g

moderate

20 mins

25 mins

 C O O K ' S   T I P

Try adding 2 finely chopped sun-dried tomatoes to the soft cheese in step 2, if you prefer.

This dish combines succulent chicken with tasty vegetables, flavoured with wine and olives.

Chicken *with* Vegetables

SERVES 4

4 chicken breasts, part boned
25 g/1 oz butter
2 tbsp olive oil
1 large onion, chopped finely
2 garlic cloves, crushed
2 peppers, red, yellow or green, halved, deseeded and cut into large pieces
225 g/8 oz large closed cup mushrooms, sliced or quartered
175 g/6 oz tomatoes, peeled and halved
150 ml/5 fl oz dry white wine
125–175 g/4–6 oz green olives, stoned
4–6 tbsp double cream
salt and pepper
pasta, to serve
chopped flat-leaved parsley, to garnish

NUTRITION

Calories 470; Sugars 7 g; Protein 29 g;
Carbohydrate 7 g; Fat 34 g; Saturates 16 g

moderate

20 mins

1 hr 30 mins

1 Season the chicken with salt and pepper to taste. Heat the oil and butter in a frying pan, add the chicken and fry until browned all over. Remove the chicken from the pan.

2 Add the onion and garlic to the frying pan and fry gently until just beginning to soften. Add the peppers to the pan with the mushrooms and continue to cook for a few minutes longer, stirring occasionally.

3 Add the tomatoes and plenty of seasoning to the pan and then transfer the vegetable mixture to an ovenproof casserole. Place the chicken on top of the bed of vegetables.

4 Add the wine to the frying pan and bring to the boil. Pour the wine over the chicken and cover the casserole tightly. Cook in a preheated oven, 180°C/350°F/Gas Mark 4, for 50 minutes.

5 Add the olives to the chicken, mix lightly then pour on the cream. Re-cover the casserole and return to the oven for 10–20 minutes or until the chicken is very tender.

6 Adjust the seasoning and serve the pieces of chicken, surrounded by the vegetables and sauce, with pasta or tiny new potatoes. Sprinkle with chopped parsley to garnish.

This casserole is packed with the sunshine flavours of Italy. Sun-dried tomatoes add a wonderful richness to the dish.

Rich Chicken Casserole

1 In a heavy or non-stick large frying pan, fry the chicken without fat over a fairly high heat, turning occasionally until golden brown. Using a slotted spoon, drain off any excess fat from the chicken and transfer the chicken to a flameproof casserole.

2 Add the olive oil to the frying pan and fry the onion, garlic and pepper over a moderate heat for 3–4 minutes. Transfer to the casserole.

3 Add the orange rind and juice, chicken stock, canned tomatoes and sun-dried tomatoes to the casserole and stir to combine.

4 Bring to the boil, then cover the casserole with a lid and simmer very gently over a low heat for about 1 hour, stirring occasionally. Add the thyme and olives, then adjust the seasoning to taste.

5 Scatter orange rind and thyme over the casserole to garnish, and serve with crusty bread.

SERVES 4

8 chicken thighs
2 tbsp olive oil
1 medium red onion, sliced
2 garlic cloves, crushed
1 large red pepper, sliced thickly
thinly pared rind and juice of 1 small orange
125 ml/4 fl oz chicken stock
400 g/14 oz canned chopped tomatoes
25 g/1 oz sun-dried tomatoes, sliced thinly
1 tbsp chopped fresh thyme
50 g/1¾ oz pitted black olives
salt and pepper
crusty fresh bread, to serve

to garnish
orange rind
thyme sprigs

NUTRITION
Calories *320*; Sugars *8 g*; Protein *34 g*;
Carbohydrate *8 g*; Fat *17 g*; Saturates *4 g*

 moderate

15 mins

1 hr 15 mins

🥄 **COOK'S TIP**

Sun-dried tomatoes have a dense texture and concentrated taste, and add intense flavour to slow-cooking casseroles.

Strips of cooked chicken are tossed with coloured pasta, grapes and carrot sticks in a delicious pesto-flavoured dressing.

Pasta *and* Chicken Medley

SERVES 2

125–150 g/4¹/₂–5¹/₂ oz dried pasta shapes, such as twists or bows
1 tbsp olive oil
2 tbsp mayonnaise
2 tsp bottled pesto sauce
1 tbsp soured cream or natural fromage frais
175 g/6 oz cooked skinless, boneless chicken meat, cut into strips
1–2 celery sticks, sliced diagonally
125 g/4¹/₂ oz black grapes (preferably seedless), halved and deseeded
1 large carrot, trimmed and cut into strips
salt and pepper
celery leaves and a few whole black grapes, to garnish

dressing
1 tbsp white wine vinegar
3 tbsp extra-virgin olive oil
salt and pepper

1 To make the dressing, whisk all the ingredients together until smooth.

2 Bring a large pan of lightly salted water to the boil, add the oil and cook the pasta for 8–10 minutes, until just tender. Drain thoroughly, rinse and drain again. Transfer to a bowl and mix in 1 tablespoon of the dressing while hot; set aside until cold.

3 Combine the mayonnaise, pesto sauce and soured cream or fromage frais in a bowl, and season to taste.

4 Add the chicken, celery, grapes, carrot and the mayonnaise mixture to the pasta, and toss thoroughly. Check the seasoning, adding more salt and pepper if necessary.

5 Arrange the pasta mixture on two plates, garnish with the celery leaves and whole black grapes and serve.

NUTRITION
Calories *609*; Sugars *11 g*; Protein *26 g*;
Carbohydrate *45 g*; Fat *38 g*; Saturates *6 g*

moderate

30 mins

10 mins

This cooking method makes the chicken aromatic and succulent, and reduces the oil needed as the chicken and vegetables cook in their own juices.

Italian Chicken Parcels

1 Cut 6 pieces of foil, each measuring about 25 cm/10 inches square. Brush the foil squares lightly with oil and set aside until required.

2 With a sharp knife, make slashes at regular intervals across each chicken breast. Slice the mozzarella cheese and place the slices between the cuts in the chicken.

3 Divide the courgettes and tomatoes between the pieces of foil and sprinkle with pepper. Tear or roughly chop the basil or oregano and scatter over the vegetables in each parcel.

4 Place the chicken on top of each pile of vegetables then wrap in the foil to enclose the chicken and vegetables, tucking in the ends.

5 Place on a baking tray and bake in a preheated oven, 200°C/400°F/Gas Mark 6, for about 30 minutes.

6 To serve, unwrap each foil parcel and serve with pasta or rice.

SERVES 4

1 tbsp olive oil
6 skinless chicken breast fillets
250 g/9 oz mozzarella cheese
500 g/1 lb 2 oz courgettes, sliced
6 large tomatoes, sliced
1 small bunch fresh basil or oregano
pepper
pasta or rice, to serve

NUTRITION
Calories 234; Sugars 5 g; Protein 28 g;
Carbohydrate 5 g; Fat 12 g; Saturates 5 g

easy

25 mins

30 mins

 COOK'S TIP

To aid cooking, put the vegetables and chicken on the shiny side of the foil so that once the parcel is wrapped the dull surface of the foil faces outwards. This ensures the heat is absorbed into the parcel and not reflected away from it.

This classic Roman dish makes an ideal light meal. It is equally good cold and could be taken on a picnic – serve with bread to mop up the juices.

Roman Chicken

SERVES 4

4 tbsp olive oil
4 chicken quarters
2 garlic cloves, crushed with 1 tsp salt
1 large red onion, sliced
4 large mixed red, green and yellow peppers, halved, deseeded and cut into strips
125 g/4½ oz stoned green olives
½ quantity Basic Tomato Sauce (see page 14)
300 ml/10 fl oz hot chicken stock
2 fresh marjoram sprigs
salt and pepper
crusty bread, to serve

1 Heat half of the oil in a flameproof casserole and brown the chicken pieces on all sides. Remove the chicken and set aside.

2 Add the remaining oil to the casserole and fry the garlic and onion until softened. Stir in the peppers, olives and Basic Tomato Sauce.

3 Return the chicken to the casserole with the stock and marjoram. Cover the casserole and simmer for about 45 minutes or until the chicken is tender. Season with salt and pepper to taste and serve with crusty bread.

NUTRITION
Calories 317; Sugars 8 g; Protein 22 g; Carbohydrate 9 g; Fat 22 g; Saturates 4 g

✪✪✪   moderate
        35 mins
        1 hr

All the sunshine colours and flavours of the Mediterranean are combined in this easy dish.

Chicken Pepperonata

1 Remove the skin from the chicken thighs and toss in the flour.

2 Heat the oil in a wide frying pan and fry the chicken quickly until sealed and lightly browned, then remove from the pan. Add the onion to the pan and gently fry until soft. Add the garlic, peppers, tomatoes and oregano, then bring to the boil, stirring.

3 Arrange the chicken over the vegetables, season well with salt and pepper, then cover the pan tightly and simmer for 20–25 minutes, or until the chicken is tender and the juices run clear when pierced with a skewer.

4 Season with salt and pepper to taste, garnish with oregano and serve with crusty wholemeal bread.

S E R V E S **4**

8 skinless chicken thighs
2 tbsp wholemeal flour
2 tbsp olive oil
1 small onion, sliced thinly
1 garlic clove, crushed
1 each large red, yellow and green peppers, halved, deseeded and sliced thinly
400 g/14 oz canned chopped tomatoes
1 tbsp chopped fresh oregano, plus extra to garnish
salt and pepper
crusty wholemeal bread, to serve

N U T R I T I O N
Calories 328; Sugars 7 g; Protein 35 g; Carbohydrate 13 g; Fat 15 g; Saturates 4 g

  easy

  15 mins

  40 mins

 C O O K ' S T I P

For extra flavour, halve the peppers and grill under a preheated grill until the skins are charred. Leave to cool, then peel and deseed. Slice the peppers thinly and use in the recipe.

The refreshing combination of chicken and orange sauce makes this a perfect dish for a warm summer evening.

Chicken *with* Orange Sauce

SERVES 4

30 ml/1 fl oz rapeseed oil
3 tbsp olive oil
4 chicken breasts about 225 g/8 oz each, boneless and skinless
150 ml/5 fl oz orange brandy
2 tbsp plain flour
150 ml/5 fl oz freshly squeezed orange juice
25 g/1 oz courgette, cut into matchstick strips
25 g/1 oz red pepper, cut into matchstick strips
25 g/1 oz leek, shredded finely
400 g/14 oz dried wholemeal spaghetti
3 large oranges, peeled and cut into segments
rind of 1 orange, cut into very fine strips
2 tbsp chopped fresh tarragon
150 ml/5 fl oz fromage frais or ricotta cheese
salt and pepper
fresh tarragon leaves, to garnish

NUTRITION

Calories 797; Sugars 28 g; Protein 59 g; Carbohydrate 77 g; Fat 25 g; Saturates 6 g

  moderate
15 mins
25 mins

1 Heat the rapeseed oil and 1 tablespoon of the olive oil in a frying pan. Add the chicken and cook quickly until golden brown. Add the orange brandy and cook for 3 minutes. Sprinkle over the flour and cook for 2 minutes.

2 Lower the heat and stir in the orange juice, courgette, pepper and leek, then season. Simmer for 5 minutes until the sauce has thickened.

3 Meanwhile, bring a saucepan of salted water to the boil. Add the spaghetti and 1 tablespoon of the olive oil and cook for 10 minutes. Drain the spaghetti, transfer to a serving dish and drizzle over the remaining oil.

4 Add half of the orange segments, half of the orange rind, the tarragon and fromage frais to the sauce in the pan and cook for 3 minutes.

5 Place the chicken on top of the pasta, pour over a little sauce, garnish with orange segments, orange rind and tarragon leaves, or other herbs if preferred. Serve immediately.

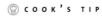 COOK'S TIP

You could use Cointreau or brandy in place of the orange brandy if this is unavailable.

Stuffed with creamy ricotta, nutmeg and spinach, the chicken is then wrapped with wafer-thin slices of Parma ham, and gently cooked in wine.

Cheese-stuffed Chicken *in* Wine

1 Put the spinach into a sieve and press out the water with a spoon. Mix with the ricotta and nutmeg and season with salt and pepper to taste.

2 Using a sharp knife, slit each chicken breast through the side and enlarge each cut to form a pocket. Fill with the spinach mixture, reshape the chicken breasts, wrap each breast tightly in a slice of ham and secure with cocktail sticks. Cover and chill in the refrigerator.

3 Heat the butter and oil in a frying pan and brown the chicken breasts for 2 minutes on each side. Transfer the chicken to a large, shallow ovenproof dish and keep warm until required.

4 Fry the onions and mushrooms for 2–3 minutes, or until lightly browned. Stir in the plain flour, then gradually add the wine and stock. Bring to the boil, stirring constantly. Season and spoon the mixture around the chicken.

5 Cook the chicken uncovered in a preheated oven, 200°C/400°F/Gas Mark 6, for 20 minutes. Turn the breasts over and cook for a further 10 minutes. Remove the cocktail sticks and serve with the sauce, together with carrot purée and green beans.

S E R V E S   4

125 g/4½ oz frozen spinach, defrosted
125 g/4½ oz ricotta cheese
pinch freshly grated nutmeg
4 skinless, boneless chicken breasts, about 175 g/6 oz each
4 Parma ham slices
25 g/1 oz butter
1 tbsp olive oil
12 small onions or shallots
125 g/4½ oz button mushrooms, sliced
1 tbsp plain flour
150 ml/5 fl oz dry white or red wine
300 ml/10 fl oz chicken stock
salt and pepper

to serve
carrot purée
green beans

N U T R I T I O N
Calories *426*; Sugars *4 g*; Protein *44 g*; Carbohydrate *9 g*; Fat *21 g*; Saturates *8 g*

  moderate

30 mins

45 mins

Served in scallop shells, this makes a stylish presentation for a starter or a light lunch.

Chicken Scallops

S E R V E S   4

175 g/6 oz short-cut macaroni, or other short
  pasta shapes
3 tbsp vegetable oil, plus extra for brushing
1 onion, chopped finely
3 rashers unsmoked collar or back bacon,
  rind removed, chopped
125 g/4½ oz button mushrooms, sliced thinly
  or finely chopped
175 g/6 oz cooked chicken, diced
175 ml/6 fl oz crème fraîche
4 tbsp dry breadcrumbs
55 g/2 oz mature Cheddar cheese, grated
salt and pepper
flat-leaved parsley sprigs, to garnish

1 Cook the pasta in a large pan of boiling salted water, with 1 tablespoon of the oil, for 8–10 minutes or until tender. Drain the pasta, return to the pan, cover and set aside.

2 Heat the grill to medium. Heat the remaining oil in a saucepan over medium heat and fry the onion until it is translucent. Add the bacon and mushrooms and cook for 3–4 minutes, stirring once or twice.

3 Stir in the pasta, chicken and crème fraîche and season to taste with salt and pepper.

4 Brush four large scallop shells with oil. Spoon in the chicken mixture and smooth to make neat mounds.

5 Mix together the breadcrumbs and cheese, and sprinkle over the top of the chicken mixture, pressing the topping lightly into the mixture. Grill for 4–5 minutes, until golden brown and bubbling. Garnish with the parsley sprigs, and serve hot.

N U T R I T I O N
Calories 532; Sugars 3 g; Protein 25 g;
Carbohydrate 33 g; Fat 34 g; Saturates 14 g

⊛⊛⊛   moderate
   20 mins
   25 mins

A rich caramelized sauce, flavoured with balsamic vinegar and wine, gives this chicken dish a piquant flavour. Serve with polenta or rice.

Chicken *with* Balsamic Vinegar

1 Using a sharp knife, make a few slashes in the skin of the chicken. Brush the chicken with the crushed garlic and place in a non-metallic dish.

2 Pour the wine and white wine vinegar over the chicken and season with salt and pepper. Cover and leave to marinate in the refrigerator overnight.

3 Remove the chicken pieces with a slotted spoon, draining well, and reserve the marinade.

4 Heat the oil and butter in a frying pan. Add the shallots and cook, stirring, for 2–3 minutes, or until they begin to soften.

5 Add the chicken pieces to the pan and cook for 3–4 minutes, turning, until browned all over. Reduce the heat and add half of the reserved marinade. Cover and cook for 15–20 minutes, adding more marinade when necessary.

6 Once the chicken is tender, add the balsamic vinegar and thyme and cook for a further 4 minutes.

7 Transfer the chicken and marinade to serving plates and serve.

SERVES 4

4 chicken thighs, boned
2 garlic cloves, crushed
200 ml/7 fl oz red wine
3 tbsp white wine vinegar
1 tbsp oil
15 g/½ oz butter
4 shallots
3 tbsp balsamic vinegar
2 tbsp fresh thyme
salt and pepper
polenta or rice, to serve

NUTRITION
Calories *148*; Sugars *0.2 g*; Protein *11 g*; Carbohydrate *0.2 g*; Fat *8 g*; Saturates *3 g*

easy

8 hrs 10 mins

35 mins

🍳 **COOK'S TIP**

To make the chicken pieces look a little neater, use wooden skewers to hold them together or secure them with a length of string.

Olives are a popular flavouring for poultry and game in the Apulia region of Italy, where this recipe originates.

Chicken *with* Green Olives

SERVES 4

3 tbsp olive oil
25 g/1 oz butter
4 chicken breasts, part boned
1 large onion, chopped finely
2 garlic cloves, crushed
2 red, yellow or green peppers, halved, deseeded and cut into large pieces
250 g/9 oz button mushrooms, sliced or quartered
175 g/6 oz tomatoes, skinned and halved
150 ml/5 fl oz dry white wine
175 g/6 oz stoned green olives
4–6 tbsp double cream
400 g/14 oz dried pasta
salt and pepper
chopped flat-leaved parsley, to garnish

NUTRITION

Calories 614; Sugars 6 g; Protein 34 g; Carbohydrate 49 g; Fat 30 g; Saturates 11 g

moderate
15 mins
1 hr 30 mins

1 Heat 2 tablespoons of the oil with the butter in a frying pan. Add the chicken breasts and fry until golden-brown all over. Remove the chicken from the pan with a slotted spoon.

2 Add the onion and garlic to the pan and fry over a medium heat until beginning to soften. Add the peppers and mushrooms and cook for 2–3 minutes. Add the tomatoes and season to taste with salt and pepper. Transfer the vegetables to a casserole and arrange the chicken on top.

3 Add the wine to the pan and bring to the boil. Pour the wine over the chicken. Cover and cook in a preheated oven, at 180°C/350°F/Gas Mark 4, for 50 minutes.

4 Add the olives to the casserole and mix in. Pour in the cream, cover and return to the oven for 10–20 minutes.

5 Meanwhile, bring a large saucepan of lightly salted water to the boil. Add the pasta and the remaining oil and cook until tender, but still firm to the bite. Drain the pasta well and then transfer to a serving dish.

6 Arrange the chicken on top of the pasta, spoon over the sauce, garnish with the parsley and serve at once. Alternatively, place the pasta in a large serving bowl and serve separately.

This Italian-style dish is richly flavoured with pesto, which is a mixture of basil, olive oil, pine nuts and Parmesan cheese.

Grilled Chicken *with* Pesto Toasts

1 Arrange the chicken in a single layer in a wide flameproof dish and brush lightly with oil. Place under a preheated grill for about 15 minutes, turning occasionally until golden brown.

2 Pierce the chicken with a skewer to make sure that there is no trace of pink in the juices.

3 Pour off any excess fat. Warm the passata and half the Pesto Sauce in a small saucepan and pour over the chicken. Grill for a few more minutes, turning until the chicken is coated.

4 Meanwhile, spread the remaining Pesto Sauce on to the slices of bread. Arrange the bread over the chicken and sprinkle with the Parmesan cheese. Scatter the pine kernels over the cheese. Grill for 2–3 minutes, or until browned and bubbling. Serve hot, garnished with a fresh basil sprig.

SERVES 4

8 part-boned chicken thighs
olive oil, for brushing
400 ml/14 fl oz passata
2 quantities of Pesto Sauce (see page 133)
12 slices French bread
85 g/3 oz freshly grated Parmesan cheese
55 g/2 oz pine kernels or flaked almonds
fresh basil sprig, to garnish

NUTRITION
Calories 787; Sugars 6 g; Protein 45 g;
Carbohydrate 70 g; Fat 38 g; Saturates 9 g

easy

10 mins

25 mins

🍲 **COOK'S TIP**

Leaving the skin on means the chicken will have a higher fat content, but many people like the rich taste and crispy skin especially when it is blackened by the barbecue. The skin also keeps in the cooking juices.

You need to put in a bit of effort to prepare the chicken, but once marinated it's a tasty candidate for the barbecue.

Barbecued Chicken

SERVES 4

1.5 kg/3 lb 5 oz whole chicken
grated rind of 1 lemon
4 tbsp lemon juice
2 fresh rosemary sprigs
1 small fresh red chilli, chopped finely
150 ml/5 fl oz olive oil

1 Split the chicken down the breast bone and open it out. Trim off excess fat, and remove the parson's nose, wing and leg tips. Break the leg and wing joints to enable you to pound it flat. This ensures that it cooks evenly. Cover the split chicken with clingfilm and pound it as flat as possible with a rolling pin.

2 Mix the lemon rind and juice, rosemary sprigs, chilli and olive oil together in a small bowl. Place the chicken in a large dish and pour over the marinade, turning the chicken to coat it evenly. Cover the dish and leave the chicken to marinate for at least 2 hours in the refrigerator.

3 Cook the chicken over a hot barbecue (the coals should be white, and red when fanned) for about 30 minutes, turning it regularly until the skin is golden and crisp. To test if it is cooked, pierce one of the chicken thighs; the juices will run clear, not pink, when it is ready. Serve.

NUTRITION
Calories 129; Sugars 0 g; Protein 22 g;
Carbohydrate 0 g; Fat 5 g; Saturates 1 g

✪✪✪   moderate
    2 hrs 30 mins
    30 mins

Chicken pieces are cooked in a succulent, mild mustard and lemon sauce, then coated in poppy seeds and served on a bed of fresh pasta shells.

Lemon Chicken Conchiglie

1 Arrange the chicken pieces, smooth- side down, in a single layer in a large ovenproof dish.

2 Mix together the butter, mustard, lemon juice, sugar and paprika in a bowl and season with salt and pepper. Brush the mixture over the upper surfaces of the chicken pieces and bake in a preheated oven, 200°C/400°F/Gas Mark 6, for 15 minutes.

3 Remove the dish from the oven and carefully turn over the chicken pieces. Coat the upper surfaces of the chicken with the remaining mustard mixture, sprinkle the chicken pieces with poppy seeds and return to the oven for a further 15 minutes.

4 Meanwhile, bring a large saucepan of lightly salted water to the boil. Add the pasta shells and olive oil and cook until tender, but still firm to the bite.

5 Drain the pasta and arrange on a warmed serving dish. Top with the chicken, then pour over the sauce and serve immediately.

SERVES 4

8 chicken pieces, about 115 g/4 oz each
55 g/2 oz butter, melted
4 tbsp mild mustard (see Cook's Tip)
2 tbsp lemon juice
1 tbsp brown sugar
1 tsp paprika
3 tbsp poppy seeds
400 g/14 oz fresh pasta shells
1 tbsp olive oil
salt and pepper

NUTRITION
Calories 652; Sugars 5 g; Protein 51 g;
Carbohydrate 46 g; Fat 31 g; Saturates 12 g

   easy

🕐 10 mins

🕐 35 mins

🍳 COOK'S TIP

Dijon is the type of mustard most often used in cooking, as it has a clean and only mildly spicy flavour. German mustard has a sweet-sour taste, with Bavarian mustard being slightly sweeter. American mustard is mild and sweet.

Napoleon's chef was ordered to cook a sumptuous meal on the eve of the battle of Marengo – this feast of flavours was the result.

Chicken Marengo

SERVES 4

8 chicken pieces, about 115 g/4 oz each
2 tbsp olive oil
300 g/10½ oz passata
200 ml/7 fl oz white wine
2 tsp dried mixed herbs
40 g/1½ oz butter, melted
2 garlic cloves, crushed
8 slices white bread
100 g/3½ oz mixed mushrooms (such as button, oyster and ceps)
40 g/1½ oz black olives, chopped
1 tsp sugar
fresh basil, to garnish

1 Using a sharp knife, remove the bone from each of the chicken pieces.

2 Heat 1 tbsp of oil in a large frying pan. Add the chicken pieces and cook for about 4–5 minutes, turning occassionally, or until browned all over.

3 Add the passata, wine and mixed herbs to the frying pan. Bring to the boil and then simmer for 30 minutes or until the chicken is tender and the juices run clear when a skewer is inserted into the thickest part of the meat.

4 Mix the melted butter and garlic together. Lightly toast the slices of bread and brush with the garlic butter.

5 Heat the remaining oil in a separate frying pan and cook the mushrooms for 2–3 minutes or until just browned.

6 Add the olives and sugar to the chicken mixture and warm through.

7 Transfer the chicken and sauce to serving plates. Serve with the bruschetta (garlic bread) and fried mushrooms.

NUTRITION
Calories 521; Sugars 6 g; Protein 47 g; Carbohydrate 34 g; Fat 19 g; Saturates 8 g

 moderate
20 mins
50 mins

🍲 **COOK'S TIP**

You can use any sort of Italian bread – ciabatta for example – to make the bruschetta, or slices of French bread.

A raspberry and honey
sauce superbly
counterbalances the
richness of the duck.

Duck *with* Raspberry Sauce

1 Trim and score the duck breasts with a sharp knife and season well all over.
Melt the butter in a frying pan, add the duck breasts and fry until lightly
coloured on all sides.

2 Add the carrots, shallots, lemon juice and half the meat stock and simmer
over a low heat for 1 minute. Stir in half the honey and half the raspberries.
Sprinkle over half the flour and cook, stirring constantly for 3 minutes.
Season with pepper to taste, then add the Worcestershire sauce.

3 Stir in the remaining stock and cook for 1 minute. Stir in the remaining
honey and remaining raspberries and sprinkle over the remaining flour.
Cook for a further 3 minutes.

4 Remove the duck breasts from the pan, but leave the sauce to continue
simmering over a very low heat, stirring occasionally.

5 Meanwhile, bring a large saucepan of lightly salted water to the boil. Add
the linguine and olive oil and cook until tender, but still firm to the bite.
Drain and divide among 4 individual plates.

6 Slice the duck breast lengthways into 5 mm-/¼ inch-thick pieces. Pour a
little sauce over the pasta and arrange the sliced duck in a fan shape on top
of it. Garnish with raspberries and flat-leaved parsley and serve.

S E R V E S 4

4 boned breasts of duck about
    275 g/9½ oz each
25 g/1 oz butter
55 g/2 oz carrots, chopped finely
55 g/2 oz shallots, chopped finely
1 tbsp lemon juice
150 ml/5 fl oz meat stock
4 tbsp clear honey
115 g/4 oz fresh raspberries, or frozen
    raspberries, thawed
25 g/1 oz plain flour
1 tbsp Worcestershire sauce
400 g/14 oz fresh linguine
1 tbsp olive oil
salt and pepper

to garnish
fresh raspberries
fresh flat-leaved parsley sprig

NUTRITION
Calories *686*; Sugars *15 g*; Protein *62 g*;
Carbohydrate *70 g*; Fat *20 g*; Saturates *7 g*

moderate
15 mins
25 mins

This scrumptious and unusual baked lasagne is virtually a meal in itself.

Pheasant Lasagne

S E R V E S   4

butter, for greasing
14 sheets pre-cooked lasagne
850 ml/1½ pints Béchamel Sauce
    (see page 14)
85 g/3 oz grated mozzarella cheese

filling
225 g/8 oz pork fat, diced
55 g/2 oz butter
16 small onions
8 large pheasant breasts, sliced thinly
25 g/1 oz plain flour
600 ml/1 pint chicken stock
1 bouquet garni
450 g/1 lb fresh peas, shelled
salt and pepper

N U T R I T I O N
Calories *1038*; Sugars *13 g*; Protein *65 g*;
Carbohydrate *54 g*; Fat *64 g*; Saturates *27 g*

✪✪✪✪   challenging
   20 mins
🕐   1 hr 15 mins

1 To make the filling, put the pork fat into a saucepan of boiling, salted water and simmer for 3 minutes, then drain and pat dry.

2 Melt the butter in a large frying pan. Add the pork fat and onions and cook for 3 minutes.

3 Remove the pork fat and onions from the pan and set aside. Add the slices of pheasant and cook over a low heat for 12 minutes, or until browned all over. Transfer to an ovenproof dish.

4 Stir the flour into the pan and cook until just brown, then blend in the stock. Pour over the pheasant, add the bouquet garni and cook in a preheated oven, 200°C/400°F/Gas Mark 6, for 5 minutes.

5 Remove the bouquet garni. Add the onions, pork fat and peas to the dish and return to the oven for 10 minutes.

6 Remove the pheasant and pork fat and process in a food precessor to mince finely.

7 Lower the oven temperature to 190°C/375°F/Gas Mark 5. Lightly grease an ovenproof dish with butter. Build layers of lasagne, minced pheasant and Béchamel Sauce in the dish, ending with Béchamel Sauce. Sprinkle over the cheese and bake in the oven for 30 minutes. Serve surrounded by the peas and onions.

Partridge has a more delicate flavour than many game birds and this subtle sauce perfectly complements it.

Lime Partridge *with* Pesto

1 Arrange the partridge pieces, smooth side down, in a single layer in a large, ovenproof dish.

2 Mix together the butter, Dijon mustard, lime juice and brown sugar in a bowl. Season to taste with salt and pepper. Brush this mixture over the uppermost surfaces of the partridge pieces and bake in a preheated oven, 200°C/400°F/Gas Mark 6, for 15 minutes.

3 Remove the dish from the oven and coat the partridge pieces with half the Pesto Sauce. Return to the oven and bake for a further 12 minutes.

4 Remove the dish from the oven and carefully turn over the partridge pieces. Coat the top of the partridges with the remaining mustard mixture and return to the oven for a further 10 minutes.

5 Meanwhile, bring a large saucepan of lightly salted water to the boil. Add the rigatoni and olive oil and cook for about 10 minutes, or until tender, but still firm to the bite. Drain and transfer to a large serving dish. Toss the pasta with the remaining Pesto Sauce and the Parmesan cheese.

6 Arrange the pieces of partridge on the serving dish with the rigatoni, then pour over the cooking juices and serve immediately.

SERVES 4

8 partridge pieces, about 115 g/4 oz each
55 g/2 oz butter, melted
4 tbsp Dijon mustard
2 tbsp lime juice
1 tbsp brown sugar
1 quantity Pesto Sauce (see page 133)
450 g/1 lb dried rigatoni
1 tbsp olive oil
115 g/4 oz freshly grated Parmesan cheese
salt and pepper

NUTRITION
Calories 895; Sugars 5 g; Protein 79 g;
Carbohydrate 45 g; Fat 45 g; Saturates 18 g

 challenging
15 mins
 40 mins

Pasta

The simplicity and satisfying nature of pasta in all its
varieties makes it a universal favourite. Easy to cook and
economical, pasta is wonderfully versatile. It can be
served with sauces made from meat, fish or vegetables, or
baked in the oven. The classic Spaghetti Bolognese needs
no introduction, and yet it is said that there are almost as
many versions of this delicious regional dish as there are
lovers of Italian food! Fish and seafood are irresistible
combined with pasta and need only the briefest of
cooking times. Pasta combined with vegetables provides
inspiration for countless dishes which will please
vegetarians and meat-eaters alike. The delicious pasta
dishes in this chapter range from easy, mid-week suppers
to elegant meals for special occasions.

The original recipe takes about 4 hours to cook and should be left overnight to allow the flavours to mingle. This version is much quicker.

Spaghetti Bolognese

SERVES 4

1 tbsp olive oil
1 onion, chopped finely
2 garlic cloves, chopped
1 carrot, scraped and chopped
1 celery stick, chopped
50 g/1¾ oz pancetta or streaky bacon, diced
350 g/12 oz lean minced beef
400 g/14 oz canned chopped tomatoes
2 tsp dried oregano
125 ml/4 fl oz red wine
2 tbsp tomato purée
salt and pepper
675 g/1½ lb fresh spaghetti or 350 g/12 oz dried spaghetti

1 Heat the oil in a large frying pan. Add the onions and cook for 3 minutes.

2 Add the garlic, carrot, celery and pancetta and sauté for 3–4 minutes or until just beginning to brown.

3 Add the beef and cook over a high heat for another 3 minutes or until all of the meat is brown.

4 Stir in the tomatoes, oregano and red wine and bring to the boil. Reduce the heat and leave to simmer for about 45 minutes.

5 Stir in the tomato purée and season with salt and pepper.

6 Cook the spaghetti in a saucepan of lightly salted boiling water for 8–10 minutes until it is tender, but still has 'bite'. Drain thoroughly.

7 Transfer the spaghetti to a serving plate and pour over the Bolognese sauce. Toss to mix well and serve hot.

NUTRITION

Calories 591; Sugars 7 g; Protein 29 g; Carbohydrate 640 g; Fat 24 g; Saturates 9 g

 easy

🕐 20 mins

🕐 1 hr 5 mins

🍴 **COOK'S TIP**

Try adding 25 g/1 oz dried porcini, soaked for 10 minutes in 2 tablespoons of warm water, to the Bolognese sauce in step 4, if you wish.

Lightly cooked eggs and pancetta are combined with cheese to make this rich, classic sauce.

Pasta Carbonara

1 Heat the oil and butter in a frying pan until it is just beginning to froth.

2 Add the pancetta or bacon to the pan and cook for 5 minutes or until browned all over.

3 Mix together the eggs and milk in a small bowl. Stir in the thyme and season with salt and pepper.

4 Cook the pasta in a saucepan of lightly salted boiling water for 8–10 minutes until tender, but still has 'bite'. Drain thoroughly.

5 Add the cooked, drained pasta to the frying pan with the eggs and cook over a high heat for about 30 seconds or until the eggs just begin to cook and set. Do not overcook the eggs or they will become rubbery.

6 Add half of the grated Parmesan cheese, stirring to combine.

7 Transfer the pasta to a warmed serving plate, pour over the sauce and toss to mix well.

8 Sprinkle the rest of the Parmesan on top and serve immediately.

SERVES 4

1 tbsp olive oil
40 g/1½ oz butter
100 g/3½ oz pancetta or unsmoked bacon, diced
3 eggs, beaten
2 tbsp milk
1 tbsp fresh thyme leaves
675 g/1½ lb fresh or 350 g/12 oz dried conchigoni rigati
50 g/1¾ oz Parmesan cheese, grated
salt and pepper

NUTRITION
Calories 547; Sugars 1 g; Protein 21 g;
Carbohydrate 49 g; Fat 31 g; Saturates 14 g

easy

15 mins

20 mins

Fresh tomatoes make a delicious Italian-style sauce which goes particularly well with pasta.

Italian Tomato Sauce *and* Pasta

SERVES 2

1 tbsp olive oil
1 small onion, chopped finely
1–2 garlic cloves, crushed
350 g/12 oz tomatoes, peeled and chopped
2 tsp tomato purée
2 tbsp water
300–350 g/10½–12 oz dried pasta shapes
90 g/3 oz lean bacon, de-rinded and diced
40 g/1½ oz mushrooms, sliced
1 tbsp chopped fresh parsley or coriander
2 tbsp soured cream or natural fromage frais (optional)
salt and pepper

1 To make the tomato sauce, heat the oil in a saucepan and fry the onion and garlic gently until soft.

2 Add the tomatoes, tomato purée, water and salt and pepper to taste to the mixture in the pan and bring to the boil. Cover, lower the heat and simmer gently for 10 minutes.

3 Meanwhile, cook the pasta in a saucepan of lightly salted boiling water for 8–10 minutes, or until just tender. Drain the pasta thoroughly and transfer to warm serving dishes.

4 Heat the bacon gently in a frying pan until the fat runs, then add the mushrooms and continue cooking for 3–4 minutes. Drain off any excess oil.

5 Add the bacon and mushrooms to the tomato mixture, together with the parsley and the soured cream, if using. Reheat and serve with the pasta.

NUTRITION
Calories *304*; Sugars *8 g*; Protein *15 g*;
Carbohydrate *31 g*; Fat *14 g*; Saturates *5 g*

⭐ very easy
🕐 10 mins
🕐 25 mins

🐾 **COOK'S TIP**

Choose any variety of pasta shape for this dish, although pasta tubes and shells are the best for holding the sauce.

The different shapes and textures of the vegetables make a mouthwatering presentation in this light and summery dish.

Broccoli *and* Asparagus Gemelli

1 Bring a large saucepan of lightly salted water to the boil. Add the pasta and olive oil and cook until tender, but still firm to the bite. Drain, return to the pan, cover and keep warm.

2 Steam the broccoli, courgettes, asparagus spears and mangetouts over a pan of boiling salted water until they are just beginning to soften. Remove from the heat and refresh in cold water. Drain and set aside.

3 Bring a small saucepan of lightly salted water to the boil. Add the frozen peas and cook for 3 minutes. Drain the peas, refresh in cold water and then drain again. Set aside with the other vegetables.

4 Put the butter and vegetable stock in a saucepan over a medium heat. Add all of the vegetables, reserving a few of the asparagus spears, and toss carefully with a wooden spoon until they have heated through, taking care not to break them up.

5 Stir in the cream and heat through without bringing to the boil. Season to taste with salt, pepper and nutmeg.

6 Transfer the pasta to a warmed serving dish and stir in the parsley. Spoon over the vegetable sauce and sprinkle over the Parmesan cheese. Arrange the reserved asparagus spears in a pattern on top and serve.

SERVES 4

225 g/8 oz dried gemelli or other pasta shapes
1 tbsp olive oil
1 head green broccoli, cut into florets
2 courgettes, sliced
225 g/8 oz asparagus spears
115 g/4 oz mangetouts
115 g/4 oz frozen peas
25 g/1 oz butter
3 tbsp vegetable stock
4 tbsp double cream
freshly grated nutmeg
2 tbsp chopped fresh parsley
2 tbsp freshly grated Parmesan cheese
salt and pepper

NUTRITION
Calories 517; Sugars 5 g; Protein 17 g;
Carbohydrate 42 g; Fat 32 g; Saturates 18 g

easy

10 mins

25 mins

A Mediterranean mixture of red peppers, garlic and courgettes cooked in olive oil and tossed with pasta.

Pasta *and* Vegetable Sauce

S E R V E S   4

3 tbsp olive oil
1 onion, sliced
2 garlic cloves, chopped
3 red peppers, halved, deseeded and cut into strips
3 courgettes, sliced
400 g/14 oz canned chopped tomatoes
3 tbsp sun-dried tomato purée
2 tbsp chopped fresh basil
225 g/8 oz fresh pasta spirals
125 g/4½ oz grated Gruyère cheese
salt and pepper
fresh basil sprigs, to garnish

1   Heat the oil in a heavy-based saucepan or flameproof casserole. Add the onion and garlic and cook, stirring occasionally, until softened. Add the peppers and courgettes and fry for 5 minutes, stirring occasionally.

2   Add the tomatoes, sun-dried tomato purée, basil and seasoning, cover and cook for 5 minutes.

3   Meanwhile, bring a large saucepan of lightly salted water to the boil and add the pasta. Stir and bring back to the boil. Reduce the heat slightly and cook, uncovered, for 3 minutes, or until just tender. Drain thoroughly and add to the vegetables. Toss gently to mix well.

4   Put the mixture into a shallow ovenproof dish and sprinkle over the cheese.

5   Cook under a preheated grill for 5 minutes until the cheese is golden. Garnish with basil sprigs and serve.

N U T R I T I O N
Calories 341; Sugars 8 g; Protein 13 g;
Carbohydrate 30 g; Fat 20 g; Saturates 8 g

very easy

15 mins

20 mins

Delicious stirred into pasta, soups and salad dressings, pesto is available in most supermarkets, but making your own gives a much fresher, fuller flavour.

Pasta *with* Classic Pesto Sauce

1 Rinse the basil leaves and pat them dry with kitchen paper.

2 Put the basil leaves, garlic, pine kernels and grated Parmesan cheese into a food processor and blend for about 30 seconds or until smooth. Alternatively, pound the ingredients by hand, using a mortar and pestle.

3 If you are using a food processor, keep the motor running and slowly add the olive oil. Alternatively, add the oil drop by drop while stirring briskly. Season with salt and pepper.

4 Meanwhile, cook the pasta in a saucepan of lightly salted boiling water according to the packet instructions, or until it is cooked through, but still has 'bite'. Drain thoroughly.

5 Transfer the pasta to a serving plate and serve with the pesto. Toss to mix well and serve hot.

SERVES 4

about 40 fresh basil leaves, washed and dried
3 garlic cloves, crushed
25 g/1 oz pine kernels
50 g/1¾ oz Parmesan cheese, finely grated
3 tbsp extra virgin olive oil
salt and pepper
675 g/1 lb 8 oz fresh pasta or 350 g/12 oz dried pasta

NUTRITION
Calories 321; Sugars 1 g; Protein 11 g; Carbohydrate 32 g; Fat 17 g; Saturates 4 g

 very easy

 15 mins

10 mins

🍳 **COOK'S TIP**

You can store pesto in the refrigerator for about 4 weeks. Cover the surface of the pesto with olive oil before sealing the container or bottle, to prevent the basil from oxidizing and turning black.

A deliciously fresh and slightly spicy tomato sauce which is excellent for lunch or a light supper.

Chilli Tagliatelle

SERVES 4

50 g/1¾ oz butter
1 onion, chopped finely
1 garlic clove, crushed
2 small fresh red chillies, deseeded and diced
450 g/1 lb fresh tomatoes, peeled, deseeded and diced
200 ml/7 fl oz vegetable stock
2 tbsp tomato purée
1 tsp sugar
salt and pepper
675 g/1 lb 8 oz fresh green and white tagliatelle, or 350 g/12 oz dried

1 Melt the butter in a large saucepan. Add the onion and garlic and cook for 3–4 minutes, or until softened.

2 Add the chillies to the pan and continue cooking for about 2 minutes.

3 Add the tomatoes and stock, then reduce the heat and leave to simmer for 10 minutes, stirring.

4 Pour the sauce into a food processor and blend for 1 minute, or until smooth. Alternatively, push the sauce through a sieve.

5 Return the sauce to the saucepan and add the tomato purée, sugar, and salt and pepper to taste. Gently reheat over a low heat, until piping hot.

6 Cook the tagliatelle in a saucepan of lightly salted boiling water according to the packet instructions, or until it is cooked, but still has 'bite'. Drain the tagliatelle, transfer to serving plates and serve with the tomato sauce.

NUTRITION

Calories *306*; Sugars *7 g*; Protein *8 g*; Carbohydrate *45 g*; Fat *12 g*; Saturates *7 g*

easy

15 mins

35 mins

🍳 COOK'S TIP

Try topping your pasta dish with 50 g/1¾ oz pancetta or unsmoked bacon, diced and dry-fried for about 5 minutes, or until crispy.

A satisfying winter dish, this pasta and bean casserole with a crunchy topping is a slow-cooked, one-pot meal.

Casseroled Beans *and* Penne

1 Put the haricot beans in a large saucepan and add sufficient cold water to cover. Bring to the boil and continue to boil vigorously for 20 minutes. Drain, set aside and keep warm.

2 Bring a large saucepan of lightly salted water to the boil. Add the penne and 1 tbsp of the olive oil and cook for about 3 minutes. Drain the pasta, set aside and keep warm.

3 Put the beans in a large, flameproof casserole. Add the vegetable stock and stir in the remaining olive oil, the onions, garlic, bay leaves, oregano, thyme, wine and tomato purée. Bring to the boil, then cover and cook in a preheated oven, 180°C/350°F/Gas Mark 4, for 2 hours.

4 Add the penne, celery, fennel, mushrooms and tomatoes to the casserole and season to taste with salt and pepper. Stir in the muscovado sugar and sprinkle over the breadcrumbs. Cover the dish and cook in the oven for 1 further hour.

5 Serve hot with salad leaves and crusty bread.

SERVES 4

225 g/8 oz dried haricot beans, soaked
    overnight and drained
225 g/8 oz dried penne
6 tbsp olive oil
850 ml/1½ pints vegetable stock
2 large onions, sliced
2 garlic cloves, chopped
2 bay leaves
1 tsp dried oregano
1 tsp dried thyme
5 tbsp red wine
2 tbsp tomato purée
2 celery sticks, sliced
1 fennel bulb, sliced
115 g/4 oz mushrooms, sliced
250 g/8 oz tomatoes, sliced
1 tsp dark muscovado sugar
4 tbsp dry white breadcrumbs
salt and pepper

to serve
salad leaves
crusty bread

NUTRITION
Calories 323; Sugars 5 g; Protein 13 g;
Carbohydrate 41 g; Fat 12 g; Saturates 2 g

⭐⭐⭐ moderate
  8 hrs 25 mins
  3 hrs 30 mins

The tasty flavours of
artichoke hearts and
black olives are a
winning combination.

Artichoke *and* Olive Spaghetti

SERVES 4

2 tbsp olive oil
1 large red onion, chopped
2 garlic cloves, crushed
1 tbsp lemon juice
4 baby aubergines, quartered
600 ml/1 pint passata
2 tsp caster sugar
2 tbsp tomato purée
400 g/14 oz can artichoke hearts, drained
   and halved
125 g/4½ oz stoned black olives
350 g/12 oz wholewheat dried spaghetti
salt and pepper
fresh basil sprigs, to garnish
olive bread, to serve

1 Heat 1 tablespoon of the oil in a large frying pan and gently fry the onion, garlic, lemon juice and aubergines for 4–5 minutes or until lightly browned.

2 Pour in the passata, season with salt and pepper to taste and add the sugar and tomato purée. Bring to the boil, then reduce the heat and simmer for 20 minutes.

3 Gently stir in the artichoke halves and olives and cook for 5 minutes.

4 Meanwhile, bring a large saucepan of lightly salted water to the boil, and cook the spaghetti for 8–10 minutes or until just tender. Drain well, toss in the remaining olive oil and season with salt and pepper to taste.

5 Transfer the spaghetti to a warmed serving bowl and top with the vegetable sauce. Garnish with basil sprigs and serve with olive bread.

NUTRITION

Calories *393*; Sugars *11 g*; Protein *14 g*;
Carbohydrate *63 g*; Fat *11 g*; Saturates *2 g*

moderate

20 mins

35 mins

🍳 COOK'S TIP

Instead of spaghetti you could use any long pasta, such as tagliatelle, pappardelle or fettuccine.

This roasted pepper and chilli pasta sauce is sweet and spicy.

Fusilli Salad *with* Chilli

1 Place the peppers, skin-side up, on a baking tray with the chilli and garlic. Cook under a preheated grill for 15 minutes, or until charred. After 10 minutes, add the tomatoes, skin-side up.

2 Place the peppers and chillies in a polythene bag and leave to sweat for 10 minutes.

3 Remove the skin from the peppers and chillies and slice the flesh into strips, using a sharp knife.

4 Peel the garlic and peel and deseed the tomatoes.

5 Place the almonds on a baking tray and toast under the grill for 2–3 minutes, or until golden.

6 Using a food processor, blend the pepper, chilli, garlic and tomatoes to make a purée. Keep the motor running and slowly add the olive oil to form a thick sauce. Alternatively, mash the mixture with a fork and beat in the olive oil, drop by drop.

7 Stir the toasted ground almonds into the mixture.

8 Warm the sauce in a saucepan until it is heated through.

9 Cook the pasta in a saucepan of lightly salted boiling water according to the packet instructions, or until it is cooked through, but still has 'bite'. Drain the pasta and transfer to a serving dish. Pour over the sauce and toss to mix. Garnish with fresh oregano leaves.

SERVES 4

2 red peppers, halved and deseeded
1 small fresh red chilli
2 garlic cloves
4 tomatoes, halved
50 g/1¾ oz ground almonds
100 ml/3½ fl oz olive oil
675 g/1 lb 8 oz fresh pasta or
   350 g/12 oz dried pasta
fresh oregano leaves, to garnish

NUTRITION
Calories *423*; Sugars *5 g*; Protein *9 g*; Carbohydrate *38 g*; Fat *27 g*; Saturates *4 g*

✪✪✪   moderate

🕙   25 mins

🕐   30 mins

This pasta dish can be prepared in a moment – the intense flavours are sure to make this a popular recipe.

Tagliatelle *and* Garlic Sauce

SERVES 4

2 tbsp walnut oil
1 bunch spring onions, sliced
2 garlic cloves, sliced thinly
225 g/8 oz mushrooms, sliced
500 g/1 lb 2 oz fresh green and
   white tagliatelle
225 g/8 oz frozen chopped leaf spinach,
   thawed and drained
125 g/4½ oz full-fat soft cheese with
   garlic and herbs
4 tbsp single cream
55 g/2 oz chopped, unsalted pistachio nuts
2 tbsp shredded fresh basil
salt and pepper
sprigs of fresh basil, to garnish
Italian bread, to serve

1 Gently heat the oil in a wok or frying pan and fry the spring onions and garlic for 1 minute or until just softened. Add the mushrooms, stir well, cover and cook gently for 5 minutes or until softened.

2 Meanwhile, bring a large saucepan of lightly salted water to the boil and cook the pasta for 3–5 minutes or until just tender. Drain the pasta thoroughly and return to the saucepan.

3 Add the spinach to the mushrooms and heat through for 1–2 minutes. Add the cheese and allow to melt slightly. Stir in the cream and continue to heat without allowing to boil.

4 Pour the mixture over the pasta, season to taste and mix well. Heat gently, stirring, for 2–3 minutes.

5 Pile into a warmed serving bowl and sprinkle over the pistachio nuts and shredded basil. Garnish with basil sprigs and serve with Italian bread.

NUTRITION
Calories 501; Sugars 3 g; Protein 15 g;
Carbohydrate 43 g; Fat 31 g; Saturates 11 g

 very easy

15 mins

20 mins

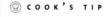 **COOK'S TIP**

Be sure to drain the spinach well before adding to the recipe.

Layers of cheese sauce, smoked cod and wholewheat lasagne can be assembled overnight and left ready to cook on the following day.

Fish *and* Vegetable Lasagne

1 Cook the lasagne in a saucepan of lightly salted boiling water until almost tender. Drain and reserve.

2 Place the smoked cod, milk, lemon juice, peppercorns, bay leaves and parsley stalks in a pan. Bring to the boil, cover and simmer for 10 minutes.

3 Lift the fish from the pan with a slotted spoon. Remove the skin and any bones. Flake the fish. Strain and reserve the liquor.

4 To make the sauce, melt the butter in a pan and fry the onion, pepper and courgette for 2–3 minutes. Stir in the flour and cook for 1 minute. Gradually add the fish liquor, then the wine, cream and prawns. Simmer for 2 minutes. Remove from the heat, add the cheese, and season.

5 Grease a shallow baking dish. Pour in a quarter of the sauce and spread evenly over the base. Cover the sauce with three sheets of lasagne, then with another quarter of the sauce.

6 Arrange the fish on top, then cover with half of the remaining sauce. Finish with the remaining lasagne, then the rest of the sauce. Sprinkle the Cheddar and Parmesan over the sauce.

7 Bake in a preheated oven, 190°C/ 375°F/Gas Mark 5, for 25 minutes, or until the top is golden brown and bubbling. Garnish and serve.

SERVES 6

8 sheets wholewheat lasagne
500 g/1 lb 2 oz smoked cod
600 ml/1 pint milk
1 tbsp lemon juice
8 peppercorns
2 bay leaves
a few fresh parsley stalks
55 g/2 oz mature Cheddar, grated
25 g/1 oz Parmesan, grated
salt and pepper
a few whole prawns, to garnish

sauce

55 g/2 oz butter, plus extra for greasing
1 large onion, sliced
1 green pepper, halved, deseeded and chopped
1 small courgette, sliced
55 g/2 oz flour
150 ml/55 fl oz white wine
150 ml/55 fl oz single cream
125 g/4½ oz shelled prawns
55 g/2 oz mature Cheddar, grated

NUTRITION

Calories *456*; Sugars *8 g*; Protein *33 g*; Carbohydrate *24 g*; Fat *24 g*; Saturates *15 g*

⭐⭐⭐   moderate
    25 mins
    50 mins

The pappardelle and vegetables are tossed in a delicious chilli and tomato sauce for a quick and economical meal.

Pasta *and* Chilli Tomatoes

SERVES 4

275 g/9½ oz pappardelle
3 tbsp groundnut oil
2 garlic cloves, crushed
2 shallots, sliced
225 g/8 oz green beans, sliced
100 g/3½ oz cherry tomatoes, halved
1 tsp chilli flakes
4 tbsp crunchy peanut butter
150 ml/¼ pint coconut milk
1 tbsp tomato purée
sliced spring onions, to garnish

1 Cook the pappardelle in a large saucepan of lightly salted boiling water for 5–6 minutes. Drain the pappardelle thoroughly and set aside.

2 Heat the groundnut oil in a large saucepan or preheated wok.

3 Add the garlic and shallots and stir-fry for 1 minute.

4 Add the green beans and drained pasta to the wok and stir-fry for 5 minutes.

5 Add the cherry tomatoes to the wok and mix well.

6 Mix together the chilli flakes, peanut butter, coconut milk and tomato purée.

7 Pour the chilli mixture over the pasta, toss well to combine and heat through, stirring.

8 Transfer to warm serving dish and garnish with spring onions. Serve immediately while still hot.

NUTRITION

Calories 353; Sugars 7 g; Protein 10 g; Carbohydrate 26 g; Fat 24 g; Saturates 4 g

very easy

15 mins

20 mins

 COOK'S TIP

Add slices of chicken or beef to the recipe and stir-fry with the beans and pasta in step 5 for a more substantial main meal.

Frozen shelled prawns can become the star ingredient in this colourful and tasty dish.

Spaghetti *and* Shellfish

1 Cook the spaghetti in a large saucepan of lightly salted boiling water, adding 1 tbsp of the oil, for 8–10 minutes or until tender. Drain, then return to the pan and stir in the remaining oil. Cover and keep warm.

2 Bring the chicken stock and lemon juice to the boil in a large saucepan. Add the cauliflower and carrots and cook for 3–4 minutes until they are barely tender. Remove with a slotted spoon and set aside. Add the mangetouts and cook for 1–2 minutes, until they begin to soften. Remove with a slotted spoon and add to the other vegetables. Reserve the stock for future use.

3 Melt half of the butter in a frying pan over a medium heat and fry the onion and courgettes for about 3 minutes. Add the garlic and prawns and cook for a further 2–3 minutes until thoroughly heated through.

4 Stir in the reserved vegetables and heat through. Season with salt and pepper, then stir in the remaining butter.

5 Transfer the spaghetti to a warmed serving dish. Pour on the sauce and parsley. Toss well using 2 forks, until thoroughly coated. Sprinkle on the grated cheese and paprika, and garnish with unshelled prawns, if using. Serve immediately.

SERVES 4

225 g/8 oz short-cut spaghetti,
  or long spaghetti broken into
  15-cm/6-inch lengths
2 tbsp olive oil
300 ml/10 fl oz chicken stock
1 tsp lemon juice
1 small cauliflower, cut into florets
2 carrots, sliced thinly
125 g/4½ oz mangetouts, trimmed
55 g/2 oz butter
1 onion, sliced
225 g/8 oz courgettes, sliced thinly
1 garlic clove, chopped
350 g/12 oz frozen shelled prawns, thawed
2 tbsp chopped fresh parsley
25 g/1 oz Parmesan, grated
salt and pepper
½ tsp paprika, to sprinkle
4 unshelled prawns, to garnish (optional)

NUTRITION
Calories 510; Sugars 38 g; Protein 33 g;
Carbohydrate 44 g; Fat 24 g; Saturates 11 g

 moderate

 20 mins

25 mins

The smoked salmon ideally complements the spaghetti to give a very luxurious dish.

Spaghetti *and* Salmon Sauce

SERVES 4

500 g/1 lb 2 oz buckwheat spaghetti
2 tbsp olive oil
90 g/3½ oz feta cheese, crumbled
coriander or parsley, to garnish

sauce
300 ml/10 fl oz double cream
150 ml/5 fl oz whisky or brandy
125 g/4½ oz smoked salmon
large pinch of cayenne pepper
2 tbsp chopped fresh coriander or parsley
salt and pepper

1 Cook the spaghetti in a large saucepan of salted boiling water, adding 1 tablespoon of the olive oil, for 8–10 minutes or until tender. Drain the pasta in a colander. Return the pasta to the pan, sprinkle over the remaining oil, cover and shake the pan. Set aside and keep warm until required.

2 In separate small saucepans, heat the cream and the whisky to simmering point. Do not let them boil.

3 Combine the cream with the whisky or brandy.

4 Cut the smoked salmon into thin strips and add to the cream mixture. Season with a little pepper and cayenne pepper to taste, and then stir in the coriander or parsley.

5 Transfer the spaghetti to a warmed serving dish, pour on the sauce and toss thoroughly using two large forks. Scatter the crumbled cheese over the pasta and garnish with the coriander or parsley. Serve at once.

NUTRITION
Calories 782; Sugars 3 g; Protein 20 g;
Carbohydrate 48 g; Fat 48 g; Saturates 27 g

very easy

10 mins

15 mins

 COOK'S TIP

You can substitute linguine, fettuccine or any other long pasta for the spaghetti, if preferred.

Serve this aromatic seafood dish with plenty of fresh crusty bread to soak up the delicious sauce.

Pasta *and* Mussel Sauce

1 Pull off the 'beards' from the mussels and rinse well in several changes of water. Discard any mussels that refuse to close when tapped. Put the mussels in a large saucepan with the white wine and half of the onions. Cover the saucepan, shake and cook over a medium heat for 2–3 minutes until the mussels have opened.

2 Remove the saucepan from the heat, lift out the mussels with a slotted spoon, reserving the liquor, and set aside until they are cool enough to handle. Discard any mussels that have not opened.

3 Melt the butter in a saucepan over medium heat and fry the remaining onion for 3–4 minutes or until translucent. Stir in the garlic and cook for 1 minute. Gradually pour on the reserved cooking liquor, stirring to blend thoroughly. Stir in the parsley and cream. Season to taste and bring to simmering point. Taste and adjust the seasoning if necessary.

4 Cook the pasta in a large saucepan of salted boiling water, with the oil, for 8–10 minutes or until tender. Drain the pasta in a colander, return to the saucepan, cover and keep warm.

5 Remove the mussels from their shells, reserving a few shells for garnish. Stir the mussels into the cream sauce. Tip the pasta into a warmed serving dish, pour on the sauce and, using 2 large spoons, toss together well. Garnish with a few of the reserved mussel shells. Serve hot, with warm, crusty bread.

SERVES 6

400 g/14 oz pasta shells
1 tbsp olive oil

sauce
3.5 litres/6 pints mussels, scrubbed
250 ml/9 fl oz dry white wine
2 large onions, chopped
125 g/4½ oz unsalted butter
6 large garlic cloves, chopped finely
5 tbsp chopped fresh parsley
300 ml/10 fl oz double cream
salt and pepper
crusty bread, to serve

NUTRITION
Calories *735*; Sugars *3 g*; Protein *37 g*;
Carbohydrate *41 g*; Fat *46 g*; Saturates *26 g*

easy

25 mins

25 mins

This Sicilian recipe of anchovies mixed with pine kernels and sultanas in a tomato sauce is delicious with all types of pasta.

Pasta *and* Sicilian Sauce

SERVES 4

50 g/1¾ oz sultanas
450 g/1 lb tomatoes, halved
25 g/1 oz pine kernels
50 g/1¾ oz canned anchovies, drained and
    halved lengthways
2 tbsp tomato purée
675 g/1 lb 8 oz fresh or
    350 g/12 oz dried penne

1 Soak the sultanas in a bowl of warm water for about 20 minutes. Drain the sultanas thoroughly.

2 Cook the tomatoes under a preheated grill for about 10 minutes. Leave to cool slightly, then once cool enough to handle, peel off the skin and dice the flesh.

3 Place the pine kernels on a baking tray and lightly toast under the grill for 2–3 minutes or until golden brown.

4 Place the tomatoes, pine kernels and sultanas in a small saucepan and gently heat through.

5 Add the anchovies and tomato purée, heating the sauce for a further 2–3 minutes or until hot. Keep warm.

6 Cook the pasta in a saucepan of salted boiling water for 8–10 minutes or until it is cooked through, but still has 'bite'. Drain thoroughly.

7 Transfer the pasta to a serving plate and serve with the hot Sicilian sauce.

NUTRITION
Calories *286*; Sugars *14 g*; Protein *11 g*;
Carbohydrate *46 g*; Fat *8 g*; Saturates *1 g*

easy

25 mins

35 mins

🍽 **COOK'S TIP**

Add 2 rashers of bacon, grilled for 5 minutes until crispy, then chopped, instead of the anchovies, if you prefer.

Fresh clams are available from most good fishmongers. If you prefer, used canned clams, which are less messy to eat, but not so pretty to serve.

Pasta *with* Clams *and* White Wine

1 If you are using fresh clams, scrub them clean and discard any that are already open.

2 Heat the oil in a large frying pan. Add the garlic and the clams to the pan and cook for 2 minutes, shaking the pan to ensure that all of the clams are coated in the oil.

3 Add the remaining seafood mixture to the frying pan and cook for a further 2 minutes.

4 Pour the wine and stock over the mixed seafood and garlic and bring to the boil. Cover the pan, reduce the heat and simmer for 8–10 minutes, or until the shells open. Discard any clams or mussels that do not open.

5 Meanwhile, cook the pasta in a saucepan of salted boiling water according to the packet instructions, or until it is cooked through, but still has 'bite'. Drain thoroughly.

6 Stir the tarragon into the sauce and season to taste.

7 Transfer the pasta to a serving plate and pour over the sauce.

SERVES 4

675 g/1 lb 8 oz fresh clams or 280 g/10 oz canned clams, drained
2 tbsp olive oil
2 garlic cloves, chopped finely
400 g/14 oz mixed seafood, such as prawns, squid and mussels, thawed if frozen
150 ml/5 fl oz white wine
150 ml/5 fl oz fish stock
675 g/1 lb 8 oz fresh pasta or
350 g/12 oz dried pasta
2 tbsp chopped fresh tarragon
salt and pepper

 COOK'S TIP

Red clam sauce can be made by adding 8 tablespoons of passata to the sauce along with the stock in step 4. Follow the same cooking method.

NUTRITION
Calories 410; Sugars 1 g; Protein 39 g; Carbohydrate 39 g; Fat 9 g; Saturates 1 g

 easy

20 mins

25 mins

This is a recipe to look forward to when parsley is at its most prolific, in the growing season.

Spaghetti, Tuna *and* Parsley

S E R V E S 4

500 g/1 lb 2 oz spaghetti
1 tbsp olive oil
25 g/1 oz butter

sauce

200 g/7 oz canned tuna, drained
55 g/2 oz canned anchovies, drained
250 ml/9 fl oz olive oil
250 ml/9 fl oz fresh flat-leaved parsley,
    chopped roughly
150 ml/ 5 fl oz crème fraîche
salt and pepper
fresh parsley, to garnish

1 Cook the spaghetti in a large saucepan of salted boiling water, with the olive oil, for 8–10 minutes or until tender. Drain the spaghetti in a colander and return to the saucepan. Add the butter, toss thoroughly to coat and keep warm until required.

2 Remove any bones from the tuna and flake into smaller pieces, using 2 forks. Put the tuna in a blender or food processor with the anchovies, olive oil and parsley and process until the sauce is smooth. Pour in the crème fraîche and process for a few seconds to blend. Taste the sauce and season.

3 Warm 4 plates. Shake the saucepan of spaghetti over a medium heat for a few minutes or until it is thoroughly warmed through.

4 Pour the sauce over the spaghetti and toss quickly, using 2 large forks. Serve immediately garnished with parsley.

N U T R I T I O N
Calories 970; Sugars 2 g; Protein 23 g;
Carbohydrate 42 g; Fat 80 g; Saturates 18 g

 moderate

 10 mins

15 mins

 C O O K ' S T I P

You can substitute any other long pasta shape for the spaghetti, if preferred.

The creamy, nutty flavour of squash complements the 'al dente' texture of the pasta perfectly. This recipe has been adapted for the microwave.

Penne *and* Butternut Squash

1 Mix together the oil, garlic and breadcrumbs and spread out on a large plate. Cook in the microwave on HIGH power for 4–5 minutes, stirring every minute, until crisp and beginning to brown. Set aside.

2 Place the squash in a large bowl with half of the water. Cover and cook on HIGH power for 8–9 minutes, stirring occasionally. Leave to stand for 2 minutes, then drain.

3 Place the pasta in a large bowl, add a little salt and pour over boiling water to cover by 2.5 cm/1 inch. Cover and cook on HIGH power for 5 minutes, stirring once, until the pasta is just tender, but still firm to the bite. Leave to stand, covered, for 1 minute before draining.

4 Place the butter and onion in a large bowl. Cover and cook on HIGH power for 3 minutes.

5 Coarsely mash the squash, using a fork. Add to the onion with the pasta, ham, cream, cheese, parsley and remaining water. Season generously and mix well. Cover and cook on HIGH power for 4 minutes until heated through.

6 Serve the pasta sprinkled with the crisp garlic crumbs.

SERVES 4

2 tbsp olive oil
1 garlic clove, crushed
55 g/2 oz fresh white breadcrumbs
500 g/1 lb 2 oz peeled, deseeded and diced butternut squash
100 ml/3½ fl oz water
500 g/1 lb 2 oz fresh penne, or other pasta shape
15 g/½ oz butter
1 onion, sliced
125 g/4½ oz ham, cut into strips
200 ml/7 fl oz single cream
55 g/2 oz Cheddar cheese, grated
2 tbsp chopped fresh parsley
salt and pepper

NUTRITION
Calories *499*; Sugars *4 g*; Protein *20 g*; Carbohydrate *49 g*; Fat *26 g*; Saturates *13 g*

⭐⭐   easy

     15 mins

     30 mins

Any variety of long pasta could be used for this very tasty dish from Sicily.

Sicilian Spaghetti Cake

SERVES 4

2 aubergines, about 650 g/1 lb 7 oz in total weight
150 ml/5 fl oz olive oil
350 g/12 oz finely minced beef
1 onion, chopped
2 garlic cloves, crushed
2 tbsp tomato purée
400 g/14 oz canned chopped tomatoes
1 tsp Worcestershire sauce
1 tsp chopped fresh oregano or marjoram or ½ tsp dried oregano or marjoram
45 g/1½ oz stoned black olives, sliced
1 green, red or yellow pepper, halved, deseeded and chopped
175 g/6 oz spaghetti
125 g/4½ oz Parmesan cheese, grated

NUTRITION
Calories 876; Sugars 10 g; Protein 37 g; Carbohydrate 39 g; Fat 65 g; Saturates 18 g

 ✪✪✪   moderate
🕐   30 mins
🕐   1 hr 10 mins

1 Brush a 20 cm/8 inch loose-based, round cake tin with olive oil, place a disc of baking parchment in the base and brush with oil. Trim the aubergines and cut into slanting slices, 5 mm/¼ inch thick. Heat some of the oil in a frying pan. Fry a few slices of aubergine at a time until lightly browned, turning once, and adding more oil as necessary. Drain on kitchen paper.

2 Put the minced beef, onion and garlic into a saucepan and cook, stirring frequently, until browned all over. Add the tomato purée, tomatoes, Worcestershire sauce, herbs and seasoning. Simmer for 10 minutes, stirring occasionally, then add the olives and pepper and cook for 10 minutes.

3 Bring a large saucepan of salted water to the boil. Cook the spaghetti for 8–10 minutes or until just tender. Drain the spaghetti thoroughly. Turn the spaghetti into a bowl and mix in the meat mixture and Parmesan, tossing together with 2 forks.

4 Lay overlapping slices of aubergine over the base of the cake tin and up the sides. Add the meat mixture, pressing it down, and cover with the remaining aubergine slices.

5 Stand the cake tin in a baking tin and cook in a preheated oven, 200°C/400°F/Gas Mark 6, for 40 minutes. Leave to stand for 5 minutes then loosen around the edges and invert on to a warmed serving dish, releasing the tin clip. Remove the baking parchment. Serve immediately.

The sauce in this delicious baked pasta dish can be used as an alternative sauce for Spaghetti Bolognese (see page 128).

Lasagne Verde

1 Begin by making the Ragù Sauce, but cook for 10–12 minutes longer than the time given, in an uncovered pan, to allow the excess liquid to evaporate. To layer the sauce with lasagne, it needs to be reduced to the consistency of a thick paste.

2 Have ready a large saucepan of boiling, salted water and add the olive oil. Drop the pasta sheets into the boiling water a few at a time, and return the water to the boil before adding further pasta sheets. If you are using fresh lasagne, cook the sheets for a total of 8 minutes. If you are using dried or partly precooked pasta, cook it according to the packet instructions.

3 Remove the pasta sheets from the saucepan with a slotted spoon. Spread them in a single layer on damp tea towels.

4 Grease a rectangular ovenproof dish, about 25–28 cm/10–11 inches long. To assemble the dish, spoon a little of the meat sauce into the prepared dish, cover with a layer of lasagne, then spoon over a little Béchamel Sauce and sprinkle with some of the cheese. Continue making layers in this way, covering the final layer of lasagne with the remaining Béchamel Sauce.

5 Sprinkle on the remaining cheese and bake in a preheated oven, 190°C/ 375°F/Gas Mark 5, for 40 minutes or until the sauce is golden brown and bubbling. Serve with a green salad, a tomato salad, or a bowl of black olives.

SERVES 6

1 quantity Ragù Sauce (see page 9)
1 tbsp olive oil
225 g/8 oz lasagne verde
1 quantity Béchamel Sauce (see page 14)
60 g/2 oz Parmesan cheese, grated
salt and pepper
green salad, tomato salad or black olives, to serve

NUTRITION
Calories 619; Sugars 7 g; Protein 29 g; Carbohydrate 21 g; Fat 45 g; Saturates 19 g

✪✪✪✪ challenging
🕐 1 hr 30 mins
🕐 1 hr

PASTA & ITALIAN

A recipe that has both Italian and Greek origins, this dish may be served hot or cold, cut into thick, satisfying squares.

Pasticcio

SERVES 6

225 g/8 oz fusilli, or other pasta shape
1 tbsp olive oil
4 tbsp double cream
salt
fresh rosemary sprigs, to garnish

sauce
2 tbsp olive oil, plus extra for brushing
1 onion, sliced thinly
1 red pepper, halved, deseeded and chopped
2 garlic cloves, chopped
625 g/1 lb 6 oz minced lean beef
400 g/14 oz canned chopped tomatoes
125 ml/4 fl oz dry white wine
2 tbsp chopped fresh parsley
50 g/1¾ oz canned anchovies, drained
    and chopped
salt and pepper

topping
300 ml/10 fl oz natural yogurt
3 eggs
pinch of freshly grated nutmeg
40 g/1½ oz Parmesan cheese, grated

NUTRITION

Calories 590; Sugars 8 g; Protein 34 g;
Carbohydrate 23 g; Fat 39 g; Saturates 16 g

easy

35 mins

1 hr 15 mins

1 To make the sauce, heat the oil in a large frying pan and fry the onion and red pepper for 3 minutes. Stir in the garlic and cook for 1 minute more. Stir in the beef and cook, stirring frequently, until the beef is no longer pink.

2 Add the tomatoes and wine, stir well and bring to the boil. Simmer, uncovered, for 20 minutes, or until the sauce is fairly thick. Stir in the parsley and anchovies, and season to taste.

3 Cook the pasta in a large pan of salted boiling water, with the oil, for 8–10 minutes or until tender. Drain the pasta in a colander, then transfer to a bowl. Stir in the cream and set aside.

4 To make the topping, beat together the yogurt and eggs and season with nutmeg, and salt and pepper to taste.

5 Brush a shallow baking dish with oil. Spoon in half of the pasta and cover with half of the meat sauce. Repeat these layers, then spread the topping evenly over the final layer. Sprinkle the cheese on top.

6 Bake in a preheated oven, 190°C/375°F/Gas Mark 5, for 25 minutes, or until the topping is golden and bubbling. Garnish with rosemary sprigs and serve.

COOK'S TIP

Serve this delicious dish with a selection of raw vegetable crudités to freshen the palate.

This variation of the traditional beef dish has layers of pasta and chicken or turkey baked in red wine, tomatoes and a delicious cheese sauce.

Chicken *and* Tomato Lasagne

1 Cook the lasagne in a pan of boiling water according to the packet instructions. Lightly grease a deep ovenproof dish.

2 Heat the oil in a pan. Add the onion and garlic and cook for 3–4 minutes. Add the mushrooms and chicken and stir-fry for 4 minutes or until the meat is browned all over.

3 Add the wine and water, bring to the boil, then simmer for 5 minutes. Stir in the passata and sugar and cook for 3–5 minutes until the meat is tender and cooked through. The sauce should have thickened, but still be quite runny.

4 To make the Cheese Sauce, melt the butter in a pan, stir in the flour and cook for 2 minutes. Remove the pan from the heat and gradually add the milk, mixing to form a smooth sauce. Return the pan to the heat and bring to the boil, stirring until thickened. Leave to cool slightly, then beat in the egg and half of the cheese. Season to taste.

5 Place 3 sheets of lasagne in the base of the dish and spread with half of the chicken mixture. Repeat the layers. Top with the last 3 sheets of lasagne, pour over the Cheese Sauce and sprinkle with the remaining Parmesan. Bake in a preheated oven, at 190°C/375°F/Gas Mark 5, for 30 minutes until the top is golden and the pasta is cooked. Serve immediately

SERVES 4

9–10 sheets of fresh lasagne or dried lasagne
1 tbsp olive oil
1 red onion, finely chopped
1 garlic clove, crushed
100 g/3½ oz mushrooms, wiped and sliced
350 g/12 oz chicken or turkey breast, cut into chunks
150 ml/5 fl oz red wine, diluted with 100 ml/3½ fl oz water
250 g/9 oz passata
1 tsp sugar

cheese sauce
75 g/2¾ oz butter
50 g/1¾ oz plain flour
600 ml/1 pint milk
1 egg, beaten
75 g/2¾ oz Parmesan cheese, grated
salt and pepper

NUTRITION
Calories 550; Sugars 11 g; Protein 35 g;
Carbohydrate 34 g; Fat 29 g; Saturates 12 g

 moderate

 20 mins

1 hr 15 mins

There is an appetizing contrast of textures and flavours in this satisfying family dish.

Tagliatelle *with* Meatballs

SERVES 4

500 g/1 lb 2 oz minced lean beef
60 g/2 oz soft white breadcrumbs
1 garlic clove, crushed
2 tbsp chopped fresh parsley
1 tsp dried oregano
large pinch of freshly grated nutmeg
1/4 tsp ground coriander
55 g/2 oz Parmesan, grated
2–3 tbsp milk
flour, for dusting
4 tbsp olive oil
400 g/14 oz tagliatelle
25 g/1 oz butter, diced
salt and pepper

sauce
3 tbsp olive oil
2 large onions, sliced
2 celery sticks, sliced thinly
2 garlic cloves, chopped
400 g/14 oz canned chopped tomatoes
125 g/4 1/2 oz sun-dried tomatoes, chopped
2 tbsp tomato purée
1 tbsp dark muscovado sugar
150 ml/5 fl oz white wine, or water

NUTRITION

Calories 910; Sugars 13 g; Protein 40 g;
Carbohydrate 65 g; Fat 54 g; Saturates 19 g

moderate

45 mins

1 hr 5 mins

1 To make the sauce, heat the oil in a frying pan and fry the onions and celery until translucent. Add the garlic and cook for 1 minute. Stir in the tomatoes, tomato purée, sugar and wine, and season. Bring to the boil and simmer for 10 minutes.

2 Meanwhile, break up the meat in a bowl with a wooden spoon until it becomes a sticky paste. Stir in the breadcrumbs, garlic, herbs and spices. Stir in the cheese and enough milk to make a firm paste. Flour your hands, take large spoonfuls of the mixture and shape it into 12 balls using your hands. Heat 3 tbsp of the oil in a frying pan and fry the meatballs for 5–6 minutes until browned.

3 Place the meatballs in a saucepan, pour the tomato sauce over, cover the saucepan and simmer on a low heat for 30 minutes, turning once or twice. Add a little extra water if the sauce begins to dry.

4 Cook the pasta in a large saucepan of salted boiling water, with the remaining oil, for 8–10 minutes or until tender. Drain the pasta, then turn into a warmed serving dish, dot with the butter and toss with two forks. Spoon the meatballs and sauce over the pasta and serve.

COOK'S TIP

Check the sauce and meatballs regularly to make sure they aren't sticking to the pan and add a little extra water to the sauce, if necessary.

These tasty little squares of pasta stuffed with mushrooms and cheese are surprisingly filling. Serve about three pieces for a starter and up to nine for a main course.

Cheesy Pasta Squares

1 Using a serrated pasta cutter, cut 5 cm/2 inch squares from the sheets of fresh pasta. To make 36 tortelloni, you will need 72 squares. Once the pasta is cut, cover the squares with clingfilm to stop them drying out.

2 Heat 25 g/1 oz of the butter in a frying pan. Add the shallots, 1 crushed garlic clove, the mushrooms and celery and cook for 4–5 minutes.

3 Remove the pan from the heat, stir in the cheese and season.

4 Spoon ½ teaspoon of the mixture on to the middle of 36 pasta squares. Brush the edges of the squares with water and top with the remaining 36 squares. Press the edges together to seal. Leave to rest for 5 minutes.

5 Bring a large saucepan of water to the boil, add the oil and cook the tortelloni, in batches, for 2–3 minutes. The tortelloni will rise to the surface when cooked and the pasta should be tender with a slight 'bite'. Remove from the pan with a slotted spoon and drain thoroughly.

6 Meanwhile, melt the remaining butter in a pan. Add the remaining garlic and plenty of pepper and cook for 1–2 minutes.

7 Transfer the tortelloni to serving plates and pour over the garlic butter. Garnish with extra grated pecorino cheese and serve immediately.

SERVES 4

about 300 g/10½ oz Basic Pasta Dough (see page 9), rolled into thin sheets
75 g/2¾ oz butter
50 g/1¾ oz shallots, chopped finely
3 garlic cloves, crushed
50 g/1¾ oz mushrooms, wiped and chopped finely
½ celery stick, chopped finely
25 g/1 oz pecorino cheese, finely grated, plus extra to garnish
1 tbsp oil
salt and pepper

NUTRITION
Calories 360; Sugars 1 g; Protein 9 g; Carbohydrate 36 g; Fat 21 g; Saturates 12 g

✪✪✪✪ challenging
  1 hr 15 mins
25 mins

Pizzas *and* Breads

Few things can beat the irresistible aroma and taste of a freshly-made pizza cooked in a wood-fired oven. The recipes for the homemade dough base and freshly made tomato sauce in this chapter will give you the closest thing possible to an authentic Italian pizza. You can add any type of topping, from salamis and cooked meats, to vegetables and fragrant herbs – the choice is yours! The Italians make delicious bread, combining all of the flavours of the Mediterranean. You can use the breads in this chapter to mop up the juices from a range of Italian dishes, or you can eat them on their own as a tasty snack.

Traditionally, pizza bases are made from bread dough; this recipe will give you a base similar to an Italian pizza.

Bread Dough Base

SERVES 2

15 g/¹⁄₂ oz fresh yeast or 1 tsp dried or easy-blend yeast
90 ml/3¹⁄₄ fl oz tepid water
¹⁄₂ tsp sugar
1 tbsp olive oil
175 g/6 oz plain flour
1 tsp salt

1 Combine the fresh yeast with the water and sugar in a bowl. If using dried yeast, sprinkle it over the surface of the water and whisk in until dissolved.

2 Leave the mixture to rest in a warm place for 10–15 minutes until frothy on the surface. Stir in the olive oil.

3 Sift the flour and salt into a large bowl. If using easy-blend yeast, stir it in at this point. Make a well in the centre and pour in the fresh yeast liquid, or water and oil (without the sugar for easy-blend yeast).

4 Using either floured hands or a wooden spoon, mix together to form a dough. Turn out on to a floured work surface and knead for about 5 minutes or until smooth and elastic.

5 Place the dough in a large greased plastic bag and leave in a warm place for about 1 hour or until doubled in size. (Airing cupboards are often the best place for this process, as the temperature remains constant.)

6 Turn out onto a lightly floured work surface and 'knock back' by punching the dough. This releases any air bubbles which would make the pizza uneven. Knead 4 or 5 times. The dough is now ready to use.

NUTRITION
Calories *182*; Sugars *2 g*; Protein *5 g*;
Carbohydrate *36 g*; Fat *3 g*; Saturates *0.5 g*

moderate

1 hr 30 mins

0 mins

This is a quicker alternative to the bread dough base. If you do not have time to wait for bread dough to rise, a scone base is ideal.

Scone Base

1 Sift the flour and salt into a large mixing bowl.

2 Rub in the butter with your fingertips until it resembles fine breadcrumbs.

3 Make a well in the centre of the flour and butter mixture and pour in nearly all of the milk at once. Mix in quickly with a knife. Add the remaining milk only if necessary to mix to a soft dough.

4 Turn the dough out onto a floured work surface and knead by turning and pressing with the heel of your hand 3 or 4 times.

5 Either roll out or press the dough into a 25-cm/10-inch circle on a lightly greased baking tray or pizza pan. Push up the edge slightly all round to form a ridge and use immediately.

SERVES 4

175 g/6 oz self-raising flour
½ tsp salt
25 g/1 oz butter
125 ml/4 fl oz milk

 COOK'S TIP

Keep utensils and ingredients as cool as possible and use a light touch for the best results, when making this scone base.

NUTRITION
Calories 215; Sugars 3 g; Protein 5 g;
Carbohydrate 35 g; Fat 7 g; Saturates 4 g

✪✪✪ moderate
20 mins
0 mins

This is an unusual pizza base made from mashed potatoes and flour and is a great way to use up any leftover boiled potatoes.

Potato Base

SERVES 4

225 g/8 oz boiled potatoes
55 g/2 oz butter or margarine
125 g/4½ oz self-raising flour
½ tsp salt

1 If the potatoes are hot, mash them, then stir in the butter until it has melted and is distributed evenly throughout the potatoes. Leave to cool.

2 Sift the flour and salt together and stir into the mashed potato to form a soft dough.

3 If the potatoes are cold, mash them without adding the butter. Sift the flour and salt into a bowl.

4 Rub in the butter with your fingertips until the mixture resembles fine breadcrumbs, then stir the flour and butter mixture into the mashed potatoes to form a soft dough.

5 Either roll out or press the dough into a 25-cm/10-inch circle on a lightly greased baking tray or pizza pan, pushing up the edge slightly all round to form a ridge before adding the topping of your choice. This potato base is rather tricky to lift before it is cooked, so you will find it much easier to handle if you roll it out directly on to the baking tray.

6 If the base is not required for cooking immediately, cover it with clingfilm and chill it for up to 2 hours.

NUTRITION
Calories 170; Sugars 1 g; Protein 4 g;
Carbohydrate 34 g; Fat 3 g; Saturates 1 g

moderate

2 hrs 15 mins

0 mins

This is a basic topping sauce for pizzas. Using canned chopped tomatoes for this dish saves time.

Tomato Sauce

1 Fry the onion and garlic gently in the oil for 5 minutes or until softened but not browned.

2 Add the tomatoes, tomato purée, sugar, oregano, bay leaf and salt and pepper to taste. Stir well.

3 Bring the sauce to the boil, cover and leave to simmer gently for 20 minutes, stirring occasionally, until you have a thickish sauce.

4 Remove the bay leaf and season to taste. Leave to cool completely before using. This sauce keeps well in a screw-top jar in the refrigerator for up to 1 week.

SERVES 4

1 small onion, chopped
1 garlic clove, crushed
1 tbsp olive oil
200 g/7 oz canned chopped tomatoes
2 tsp tomato purée
½ tsp sugar
½ tsp dried oregano
1 bay leaf
salt and pepper

NUTRITION
Calories 41; Sugars 3 g; Protein 1 g;
Carbohydrate 3 g; Fat 3 g; Saturates 0.4 g

moderate

5 mins

25 mins

COOK'S TIP

You can use fresh tomatoes for this dish, if you prefer, but choose ripe plum tomatoes and increase the cooking time so that the sauce thickens nicely and the tomatoes soften enough.

PASTA & ITALIAN

This sauce is made with fresh tomatoes. Use the plum variety whenever available and always choose the reddest ones for the best flavour.

Special Tomato Sauce

SERVES 4

1 small onion, chopped
1 small red pepper, chopped
1 garlic clove, crushed
2 tbsp olive oil
225 g/8 oz tomatoes
1 tbsp tomato purée
1 tsp soft brown sugar
2 tsp chopped fresh basil
½ tsp dried oregano
1 bay leaf
salt and pepper

1 Fry the onion, pepper and garlic gently in the oil for 5 minutes until softened, but not browned.

2 Cut a cross in the base of each tomato and place them in a bowl. Pour on boiling water and leave for about 45 seconds. Drain, and then plunge in cold water. The skins will slide off easily.

3 Chop the tomatoes, discarding any hard cores.

4 Add the tomatoes to the onion mixture with the tomato purée, sugar, herbs and seasoning. Stir well. Bring to the boil, cover and leave to simmer gently for about 30 minutes, stirring occasionally, or until you have a thickish sauce.

5 Remove the bay leaf and adjust the seasoning to taste. Leave to cool completely before using.

6 This sauce will keep in a screw-top jar in the refrigerator for up to 1 week.

NUTRITION
Calories *81*; Sugars *6 g*; Protein *1 g*;
Carbohydrate *6 g*; Fat *6 g*; Saturates *1 g*

moderate

 10 mins

35 mins

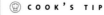 **COOK'S TIP**

As an alternative method of skinning tomatoes, hold the tomato over a naked flame, using a fork, until the tomato skin blisters, when it should come off easily.

Pizza means 'pie' in Italian. The fresh bread dough is not difficult to make, but it does take a little time.

Pizza Margarita

1 Place the yeast and sugar in a measuring jug and mix with 50 ml/2 fl oz of the water. Leave the yeast mixture in a warm place for 15 minutes, or until it is frothy.

2 Mix the salt with the flour in a bowl and make a well in the centre. Add the oil, the yeast mixture and the remaining water. Using a wooden spoon, mix to form a dough.

3 Turn the dough out on to a floured surface and knead for 4–5 minutes, or until smooth.

4 Return the dough to the bowl, cover with an oiled sheet of clingfilm and leave to rise for 30 minutes, or until doubled in size.

5 Knead the dough for 2 minutes. Stretch the dough with your hands, then place it on an oiled baking tray, pushing out the edges until even and to the shape required. The dough should be no more than 5 mm/¼ inch thick because it will rise during cooking.

6 To make the topping, place the tomatoes, garlic, dried basil, olive oil and salt and pepper to taste in a large frying pan and leave to simmer for about 20 minutes, or until the sauce has thickened. Stir in the tomato purée and leave to cool slightly.

7 Spread the topping evenly over the pizza base. Top with the mozzarella and Parmesan cheeses and bake in a preheated oven at 200°C/400°F/Gas Mark 6, for about 20–25 minutes. Serve hot.

SERVES 4

basic pizza dough
10 g/¼ oz dried yeast
1 tsp sugar
250 ml/9 fl oz hand-hot water
1 tsp salt
350 g/12 oz strong plain flour
1 tbsp olive oil

topping
400 g/14 oz canned tomatoes, chopped
2 garlic cloves, crushed
2 tsp dried basil
1 tbsp olive oil
2 tbsp tomato purée
100 g/3½ oz mozzarella cheese, chopped
2 tbsp freshly grated Parmesan cheese
salt and pepper

NUTRITION
Calories 456; Sugars 7 g; Protein 16 g;
Carbohydrate 74 g; Fat 13 g; Saturates 5 g

 moderate

1 hr

 45 mins

Wonderfully colourful vegetables are roasted in olive oil with thyme and garlic. The goat's cheese adds a nutty, piquant flavour.

Vegetable *and* Goat's Cheese Pizza

SERVES 4

2 baby courgettes, halved lengthways
2 baby aubergines, quartered lengthways
½ red pepper, cut into 4 strips
½ yellow pepper, cut into 4 strips
1 small red onion, cut into wedges
2 garlic cloves, unpeeled
4 tbsp olive oil
1 tbsp red wine vinegar
1 tbsp chopped fresh thyme
1 quantity Bread Dough Base (see page 156)
1 quantity Special Tomato Sauce (see page 160)
90 g/3¼ oz goat's cheese
salt and pepper
fresh basil leaves, to garnish

1 Place all of the prepared vegetables and garlic in a large roasting tin. Mix together the olive oil, vinegar, thyme and plenty of seasoning and pour over, coating well.

2 Roast the vegetables in a preheated oven, at 200°C/400°F/Gas Mark 6, for 15–20 minutes or until the skins have started to blacken in places, turning half-way through. Leave to rest for 5 minutes after roasting.

3 Carefully peel off the skins from the roast peppers and the garlic cloves. Slice the garlic.

4 Roll out or press the dough, using a rolling pin or your hands, into a 25 cm/ 10 inch circle on a lightly floured work surface. Place on a large greased baking tray or pizza pan and raise the edge a little. Cover and leave for 10 minutes to rise slightly in a warm place. Spread with the tomato sauce almost to the edge.

5 Arrange the roasted vegetables on top and dot with the cheese. Drizzle the oil and juices from the roasting tin over the pizza and season.

6 Bake in a preheated oven, at 200°C/400°F/Gas Mark 6, for 18–20 minutes, or until the edge is crisp and golden. Serve immediately, garnished with fresh basil leaves.

NUTRITION
Calories *387*; Sugars *9 g*; Protein *10 g*;
Carbohydrate *42 g*; Fat *21 g*; Saturates *5 g*

moderate

2 hrs 30 mins

40 mins

Juicy mushrooms and stringy mozzarella top this tomato-based pizza. Use wild mushrooms or a combination of wild and cultivated mushrooms.

Mushroom Pizza

1 Knead the dough for 2 minutes. Using a rolling pin, roll out the dough to form an oval or a circular shape, then place it on an oiled baking tray, pushing out the edges until even. The dough should be no more than 5 mm/¼ inch thick because it will rise during cooking.

2 To make the topping, place the tomatoes, garlic, dried basil, olive oil and salt and pepper in a large pan and simmer for 20 minutes, or until the sauce has thickened. Stir in the tomato purée and leave to cool slightly.

3 Spread the sauce evenly over the base of the pizza, top with the sliced mushrooms and scatter over the grated mozzarella.

4 Bake in a preheated oven, at 200°C/400°F/Gas Mark 6, for 25 minutes. Just before serving, garnish with fresh basil leaves.

S E R V E S   **4**

1 quantity Basic Pizza Dough (see page 161)

topping
400g/14 oz canned chopped tomatoes
2 garlic cloves, crushed
1 tsp dried basil
1 tbsp olive oil
2 tbsp tomato purée
200 g/7 oz mushrooms, sliced
150 g/5½ oz mozzarella cheese, grated
salt and pepper
fresh basil leaves, to garnish

N U T R I T I O N
Calories *302*; Sugars *7 g*; Protein *10 g*;
Carbohydrate *41 g*; Fat *12 g*; Saturates *4 g*

★★★   moderate
🕐   1 hr 15 mins
🕐   45 mins

👨‍🍳 **C O O K ' S   T I P**

You can just as easily make smaller, individual pizzas – simply reduce the cooking time slightly.

The vibrant colours of the peppers and onion make this a delightful pizza. Served cut into fingers, it is ideal for a party or buffet.

Californian Pepper Pizza

SERVES 8

1 quantity Bread Dough Base (see page 156)
2 tbsp olive oil
½ each red, green and yellow peppers, deseeded and sliced thinly
1 small red onion, sliced thinly
1 garlic clove, crushed
1 quantity Special Tomato Sauce (see page 160)
3 tbsp raisins
25 g/1 oz pine kernels
1 tbsp chopped fresh thyme
olive oil, for drizzling
salt and pepper

1 Roll out or press the dough, using a rolling pin or your hands, on a lightly floured work surface to fit a 30 x 18-cm/12 x 7-inch greased Swiss roll tin . Place the dough in the tin and push up the edges slightly.

2 Cover and leave the dough to rise slightly in a warm place for about 10 minutes.

3 Heat the oil in a large frying pan. Add the peppers, onion and garlic, and fry gently for 5 minutes until they have softened, but not browned. Leave to cool slightly.

4 Spread the tomato sauce over the base of the pizza almost to the edge.

5 Sprinkle over the raisins and top with the cooled pepper mixture. Add the pine kernels and thyme. Drizzle with a little olive oil and season well.

6 Bake in a preheated oven, at 200°C/400°F/Gas Mark 6, for 18–20 minutes, or until the edges are crisp and golden. Cut into fingers and serve immediately.

NUTRITION
Calories 380; Sugars 19 g; Protein 7 g;
Carbohydrate 53 g; Fat 17 g; Saturates 2 g

moderate

2 hrs 30 mins

25 mins

As the name implies, this colourful pizza should be topped with fresh vegetables from the garden, especially in the summer months.

Giardiniera Pizza

1 Remove any tough stalks from the spinach and wash the leaves in cold water. Pat dry with kitchen paper.

2 Roll out or press the potato base, using a rolling pin or your hands, into a large 25-cm/10-inch circle on a lightly floured work surface. Place the round on a large greased baking tray or pizza pan and push up the edge a little. Spread with the tomato sauce.

3 Arrange the spinach leaves on the sauce, followed by the tomato slices. Top with the remaining vegetables and the herbs.

4 Mix together the cheeses and sprinkle over. Place the artichoke heart in the centre. Drizzle the pizza with a little olive oil and season.

5 Bake in a preheated oven, at 200°C/400°F/Gas Mark 6, for 18–20 minutes, or until the edges are crisp and golden brown. Serve immediately.

SERVES 4

6 spinach leaves
1 quantity Potato Base (see page 158)
1 quantity Special Tomato Sauce (see page 160)
1 tomato, sliced
1 celery stick, sliced thinly
½ green pepper, sliced thinly
1 baby courgette, sliced
25 g/1 oz asparagus tips
25 g/1 oz sweetcorn, thawed if frozen
25 g/1 oz peas, thawed if frozen
4 spring onions, trimmed and chopped
1 tbsp chopped fresh mixed herbs
55 g/2 oz mozzarella, grated
2 tbsp freshly grated Parmesan cheese
1 artichoke heart
olive oil, for drizzling
salt and pepper

NUTRITION
Calories *362*; Sugars *10 g*; Protein *13 g*; Carbohydrate *48 g*; Fat *15 g*; Saturates *5 g*

     moderate
2 hrs 30 mins
20 mins

⊕ COOK'S TIP

Use any mixture of fresh herbs for this pizza. Good combinations are basil, parsley and mint or oregano, parsley and thyme.

This is a traditional dish
from the Calabrian
Mountains in southern
Italy, where it is made
with naturally sun-dried
tomatoes and
ricotta cheese.

Sun-dried Tomato *and* Ricotta Pizza

SERVES 4

1 quantity Basic Pizza Dough (see page 161)

topping
4 tbsp sun-dried tomato purée
150g/5½ oz ricotta cheese
10 sun-dried tomatoes, cut into strips
1 tbsp fresh thyme
salt and pepper

1 Using a rolling pin, roll out the dough to form a circle, then place it on an oiled baking tray, pushing out the edges until even. The dough should be no more than 6 mm/¼ inch thick because it will rise during cooking.

2 Spread the sun-dried tomato paste over the dough, then add spoonfuls of ricotta cheese.

3 Arrange the sun-dried tomatoes on top.

4 Sprinkle the thyme and salt and pepper to taste over the top of the pizza. Bake in a preheated oven, at 200°C/400°F/Gas Mark 6, for 30 minutes or until the crust is golden. Serve hot.

NUTRITION
Calories *274*; Sugars *4 g*; Protein *8 g*;
Carbohydrate *38 g*; Fat *11 g*; Saturates *4 g*

⊛⊛⊛ moderate
🕐 1hr 15 mins
🕐 30 mins

 COOK'S TIP

As an alternative to the ricotta cheese, use any soft cream cheese or creamy goat's cheese, which goes beautifully with sun-dried tomatoes.

A pizza adaptation of Eggs Florentine – sliced hard-boiled eggs on freshly cooked spinach, with a crunchy almond topping.

Florentine Pizza

1 Mix the Parmesan with the potato base. Roll out or press the dough, using a rolling pin or your hands, into a 25-cm/10-inch circle on a lightly floured work surface. Place on a large greased baking tray or pizza pan and push up the edge slightly. Spread the tomato sauce almost to the edge.

2 Remove the stalks and wash the spinach leaves thoroughly in plenty of cold water. Drain well and pat off the excess water with kitchen paper.

3 Fry the onion gently in the oil for 5 minutes or until softened. Add the spinach and continue to fry until just wilted. Drain off any excess liquid. Arrange on the pizza and sprinkle over the nutmeg.

4 Remove the shells from the eggs and slice. Arrange the slices of egg on top of the spinach.

5 Mix together the breadcrumbs, cheese and almonds, and sprinkle over the top. Drizzle a little olive oil over the pizza and season with salt and pepper.

6 Bake in a preheated oven, at 200°C/400°F/Gas Mark 6, for 18–20 minutes, or until the edge is crisp and golden. Serve immediately.

SERVES 4

2 tbsp freshly grated Parmesan cheese
1 quantity Potato Base (see page 158)
1 quantity Special Tomato Sauce (see page 160)
175 g/6 oz spinach
1 small red onion, sliced thinly
2 tbsp olive oil
1/4 tsp freshly grated nutmeg
2 hard-boiled eggs
15 g/1/2 oz fresh white breadcrumbs
55 g/2 oz Jarlsberg cheese, grated (or Cheddar or Gruyère cheese, if unavailable)
2 tbsp flaked almonds
olive oil, for drizzling
salt and pepper

NUTRITION
Calories 462; Sugars 6 g; Protein 18 g; Carbohydrate 41 g; Fat 26 g; Saturates 8 g

✪✪✪ moderate
 2 hrs 30 mins
🕐 25 mins

This is a traditional pizza on which the toppings are divided into four sections, each of which is supposed to depict a season of the year.

Four Seasons Pizza

SERVES 4

1 quantity Bread Dough Base (see page 156)
1 quantity Special Tomato Sauce (see page 160)
25 g/1 oz chorizo sausage, sliced thinly
25 g/1 oz button mushrooms, wiped and sliced thinly
45 g/1½ oz artichoke hearts, sliced thinly
25 g/1 oz mozzarella, sliced thinly
3 anchovies, halved lengthways
2 tsp capers
4 pitted black olives, sliced
4 fresh basil leaves, shredded
olive oil, for drizzling
salt and pepper

1 Roll out or press the dough, using a rolling pin or your hands, into a 25-cm/ 10-inch circle on a lightly floured surface. Place on a large greased baking tray or pizza pan and push up the edge a little.

2 Cover and leave to rise slightly for 10 minutes in a warm place. Spread the tomato sauce over the pizza base, almost to the edge.

3 Put the sliced chorizo on to one quarter of the pizza, the sliced mushrooms on another, the artichoke hearts on a third, and the mozzarella and anchovies on the fourth.

4 Dot all over with the capers, olives and basil leaves. Drizzle with a little olive oil and season with salt and pepper. Do not put any salt on the anchovy section as the fish are very salty.

5 Bake in a preheated oven, at 200°C/400°F/Gas Mark 6, for 18–20 minutes, or until the crust is golden and crisp. Serve immediately.

NUTRITION
Calories *313*; Sugars *8 g*; Protein *8 g*; Carbohydrate *44 g*; Fat *13 g*; Saturates *3 g*

moderate

2 hrs 45 mins

20 mins

An unusual fragrant, spiced pizza topped with minced lamb and aubergine on a bread base.

Aubergine *and* Lamb Pizza

1 Place the diced aubergine in a colander, sprinkle with the salt and let the bitter juices drain for about 20 minutes. Rinse thoroughly, then pat dry with kitchen paper.

2 Roll out or press the dough, using a rolling pin or your hands, into a 25-cm/ 10-inch circle on a lightly floured work surface. Place on a large greased baking tray or pizza pan and push up the edge to form a rim.

3 Cover and leave to rise slightly for 10 minutes in a warm place.

4 Fry the onion, garlic and cumin seeds gently in the oil for 3 minutes. Increase the heat slightly and add the lamb, aubergine and pimiento. Fry for 5 minutes, stirring occasionally. Add the coriander and season with salt and pepper to taste.

5 Spread the tomato sauce over the dough base, almost to the edge. Top with the lamb mixture.

6 Arrange the mozzarella slices on top. Drizzle over a little olive oil and season with salt and pepper.

7 Bake in a preheated oven, at 200°C/400°F/Gas Mark 6, for 18–20 minutes, or until the crust is crisp and golden. Serve immediately.

SERVES 4

1 small aubergine, diced
1 quantity Bread Dough Base (see page 156)
1 tbsp olive oil
1 small onion, sliced thinly
1 garlic clove, crushed
1 tsp cumin seeds
175 g/6 oz minced lamb
25 g/1 oz canned pimiento, sliced thinly
2 tbsp chopped fresh coriander
1 quantity Special Tomato Sauce
  (see page 160)
90 g/3 oz mozzarella, sliced thinly
olive oil, for drizzling
salt and pepper

NUTRITION
Calories 430; Sugars 10 g; Protein 18 g;
Carbohydrate 44 g; Fat 22 g; Saturates 7 g

 moderate

 2 hrs 30 mins

30 mins

This more traditional kind of pizza is topped with pepperoni, smoked bacon and peppers and covered in a smoked cheese.

Smoky Bacon *and* Pepperoni Pizza

SERVES 4

1 quantity Bread Dough Base (see page 156)
1 tbsp olive oil
1 tbsp freshly grated Parmesan cheese
1 quantity Special Tomato Sauce
  (see page 160)
125 g/4½ oz lightly smoked bacon, diced
½ green pepper, sliced thinly
½ yellow pepper, sliced thinly
55 g/2 oz pepperoni-style sliced spicy
  sausage
55 g/2 oz smoked Bavarian cheese, grated
½ tsp dried oregano
olive oil, for drizzling
salt and pepper

1 Roll out or press the dough, using a rolling pin or your hands, into a 25-cm/10-inch circle on a lightly floured work surface.

2 Place the dough base on a large greased baking tray or pizza pan and push up the edge a little with your fingers, to form a rim.

3 Brush the base with the olive oil and sprinkle with the Parmesan. Cover and leave to rise slightly in a warm place for about 10 minutes.

4 Spread the tomato sauce over the base almost to the edge. Top with the bacon and peppers. Arrange the pepperoni on top and sprinkle with the smoked cheese.

5 Sprinkle over the oregano and drizzle with a little olive oil. Season well.

6 Bake in a preheated oven, at 200°C/400°F/Gas Mark 6, for 18–20 minutes, or until the crust is golden and crisp around the edge. Cut the pizza into wedges and serve immediately.

NUTRITION
Calories 450; Sugars 6 g; Protein 19 g;
Carbohydrate 41 g; Fat 24 g; Saturates 6 g

moderate

1 hr 30 mins

20 mins

This pizza is topped with a cocktail of mixed seafood, such as prawns, mussels, cockles and squid.

Marinara Pizza

1 Roll out or press out the potato dough, using a rolling pin or your hands, into a 25-cm/10-inch circle on a lightly floured work surface.

2 Place the dough on a large greased baking tray or pizza pan and push up the edge a little with your fingers to form a rim.

3 Spread the tomato sauce evenly over the base almost to the edge.

4 Arrange the seafood cocktail, capers and yellow pepper on top of the tomato sauce.

5 Sprinkle over the herbs and cheeses. Arrange the olives on top. Drizzle over a little olive oil and season with salt and pepper to taste.

6 Bake in a preheated oven, at 200°C/400°F/Gas Mark 6, for 18–20 minutes or until the edge of the pizza is crisp and golden brown.

7 Transfer to a warmed serving plate, garnish with a sprig of marjoram or oregano and serve immediately.

SERVES 4

1 quantity Potato Base (see page 158)
1 quantity Special Tomato Sauce (see page 160)
200 g/7 oz frozen seafood cocktail, thawed
1 tbsp capers
1 small yellow pepper, chopped
1 tbsp chopped fresh marjoram
½ tsp dried oregano
55 g/2 oz mozzarella, grated
15 g/½ oz Parmesan cheese, grated
12 black olives
olive oil, for drizzling
salt and pepper
sprig of fresh marjoram or oregano, to garnish

NUTRITION
Calories 359; Sugars 9 g; Protein 19 g; Carbohydrate 42 g; Fat 14 g; Saturates 4 g

⭐⭐⭐ moderate

🕒 2 hrs 30 mins

🕐 20 mins

COOK'S TIP

You can use a selection of fresh seafood, such as peeled prawns, cooked squid, and shelled mussels and cockles.

This is a variation of the classic Italian pizza, but it is made with ready-made puff pastry. It is perfect for al fresco eating.

Pissaladière

SERVES 4

4 tbsp olive oil, plus extra for greasing
700 g/1 lb 9 oz red onions, sliced thinly
2 garlic cloves, crushed
2 tsp caster sugar
2 tbsp red wine vinegar
350 g/12 oz fresh ready-made puff pastry
salt and pepper

topping
2 x 50 g/1¾ oz canned anchovy fillets
12 green stoned olives
1 tsp dried marjoram

1 Lightly grease a Swiss roll tin. Heat the olive oil in a large saucepan. Add the red onions and garlic and cook over a low heat for about 30 minutes, stirring from time to time.

2 Add the sugar and red wine vinegar to the saucepan and season with plenty of salt and pepper.

3 On a lightly floured surface, roll out the pastry to a rectangle, about 33 x 23 cm/13 x 9 inches. Place the pastry rectangle on to the prepared tin, pushing the pastry into the corners of the tin.

4 Spread the onion mixture evenly over the pastry.

5 Arrange the anchovy fillets and green olives on top, then sprinkle all over with the marjoram.

6 Bake in a preheated oven, at 220°C/425°F/Gas Mark 7, for 20–25 minutes or until the pissaladière is lightly golden. Serve the pissaladière piping hot, straight from the oven.

NUTRITION
Calories 612; Sugars 13 g; Protein 12 g;
Carbohydrate 47 g; Fat 43 g; Saturates 11 g

 easy

20 mins

55 mins

🍳 **COOK'S TIP**

Cut the pissaladière into squares or triangles for easy-to-eat finger food at a party or barbecue.

These pizza dough Italian pasties are best served hot with a salad for a delicious lunch or supper dish.

Potato *and* Tomato Calzone

1 To make the dough, sift the flour into a large mixing bowl and stir in the yeast. Make a well in the centre of the mixture. Stir in the vegetable stock, honey and caraway seeds and bring the mixture together to form a dough.

2 Turn the dough out on to a lightly floured surface and knead for 8 minutes until smooth. Place the dough in a lightly oiled mixing bowl, cover and leave to rise in a warm place for 1 hour or until it has doubled in size.

3 Meanwhile, make the filling. Heat the oil in a frying pan and add all the remaining ingredients except for the cheese. Cook for about 5 minutes, stirring occasionally.

4 Divide the risen dough into 4 pieces. On a lightly floured surface, roll them out to form 4 x 18-cm/7-inch circles. Spoon equal amounts of the filling on to one half of each circle. Sprinkle the cheese over the filling. Brush the edge of the dough with milk and fold the dough over to form 4 semi-circles, pressing to seal the edges.

5 Place on a non-stick baking tray and brush with milk. Cook in a preheated oven, 220°C/425°F/Gas Mark 7, for 30 minutes, until golden and risen.

SERVES **4**

dough
450 g/1 lb plain white bread flour
1 tsp easy blend dried yeast
300 ml/10 fl oz warm vegetable stock
1 tbsp clear honey
1 tsp caraway seeds
skimmed milk, for glazing

filling
1 tbsp vegetable oil
225 g/8 oz waxy potatoes, diced
1 onion, halved and sliced
2 garlic cloves, crushed
40 g/1½ oz sun-dried tomatoes
2 tbsp chopped fresh basil
2 tbsp tomato purée
2 celery sticks, sliced
50 g/1¾ oz mozzarella cheese, grated

NUTRITION
Calories *524*; Sugars *8 g*; Protein *17 g*;
Carbohydrate *103 g*; Fat *8 g*; Saturates *2 g*

　moderate
　1 hr 30 mins
　35 mins

Index